MAKING HISTORY
HOW TO CREATE A HISTORICAL WEB SITE

Center for History and New Media at George Mason University
for National History Day

Another title in the NHD "Making History: How To" series.

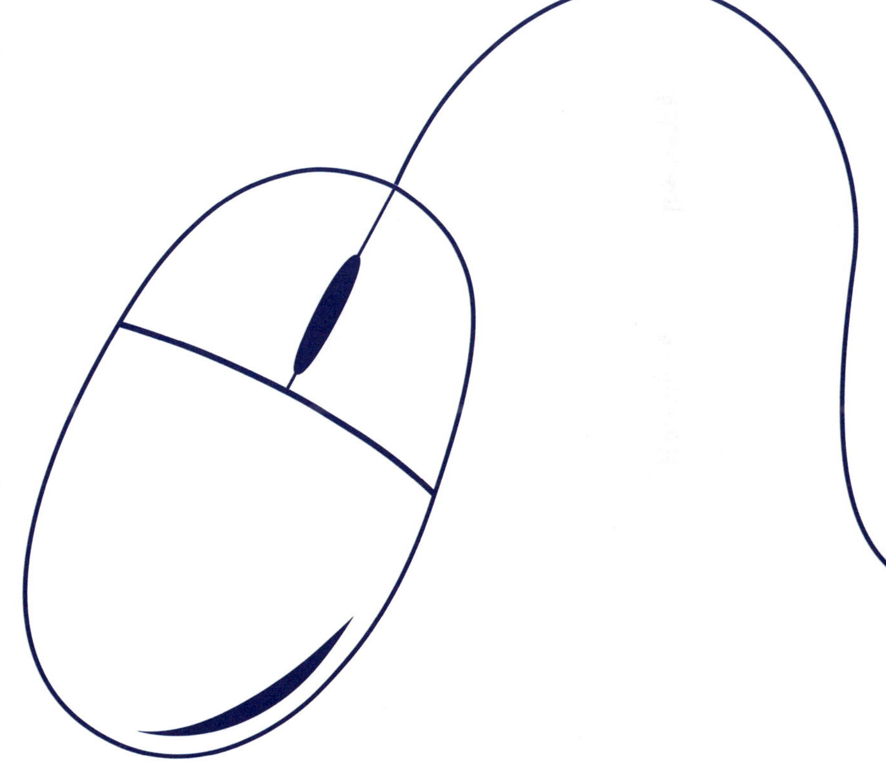

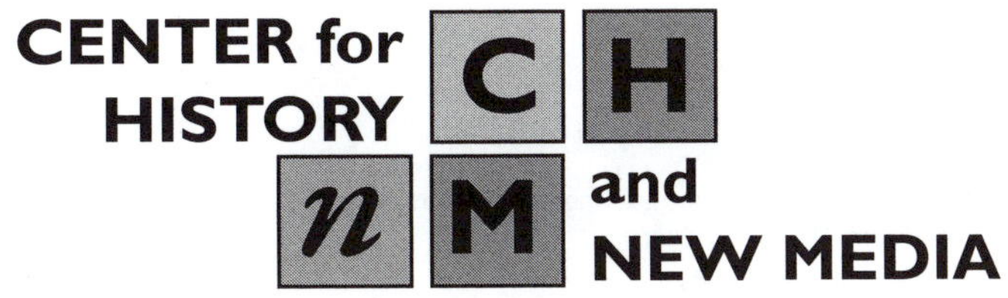

Dear Teachers, Parents, and Students,

On behalf of National History Day (NHD), I am pleased to introduce Making History, *a series of instructional materials designed to improve student research and presentation of historical projects through their involvement in the NHD program.*

The Making History *series is composed of* A Guide to Historical Research through the National History Day Program *for teachers and a set of five student-focused guidebooks, each designed to direct students in producing creative historical presentations through exhibits, documentaries, performances, traditional research papers, or Web sites. NHD collaborated with representatives of five nationally recognized organizations, who shared their expertise in the following areas.*

How to Create a Historical Exhibit

Developed by the National Archives and Records Administration, this book guides students through the process of exhibit design, following the same criteria professional museum designers use to create a museum exhibit. Examples of professional exhibits and award-winning NHD student exhibits are included.

How to Create a Historical Documentary

In the guide and accompanying DVD, the History Channel takes students through the process of documentary production. Tips on storyboarding, credits, and visual impact are provided.

How to Create a Historical Performance

In this guide and DVD, experts at The Colonial Williamsburg Foundation highlight the key areas to consider in developing a historical performance and offer tips on script writing, choosing props and costumes, and developing a character. Sample award-winning NHD student performances are included on the DVD.

How to Create a Historical Paper

Our friends at the Newsweek Education Program take students from researching a topic through the writing process and explain the most effective way to write a coherent, organized, interesting historical essay.

How to Create a Historical Web Site

Developed by the Center for History and New Media at George Mason University, this guide teaches students the process of Web site development and presentation while maintaining quality historical content and originality.

I am indebted to our partners for sharing their expertise and to the Winter Group for the series' beautiful design. My special thanks to ABC-CLIO for providing expert editorial and production assistance.

I hope you find the content clear and user friendly and the authorship unrivaled.

Cathy Gorn
Executive Director
National History Day
August 2008

National History Day

For more information about NHD, go to www.nhd.org

For more information about our partners and to discover more about their own educational offerings, visit:

www.history.org | www.nara.gov | www.abc-clio.com
www.historychannel.com | www.chnm.gmu.edu

Library of Congress Cataloging-in-Publication Data
How to create a historical web site. — 1st ed.
p. cm.
"NHD 'making history, how to' series."
Includes bibliographical references.
ISBN 978-0-9790266-1-4 (alk. paper)
1. Web sites--Design—Handbooks, manuals, etc. 2. Web site development—Handbooks, manuals, etc. 3. United States—History—Computer networks.
4. World history—Computer networks. I. National History Day (Organization)
TK5105.888.H659 2008
006.7—dc22

2008043964

CONTENTS

INTRODUCTION

Congratulations! You are on your way to producing your own history Web site for National History Day. This experience will be a good opportunity to research and analyze a historical topic and to design and build a history Web site.

This guide will teach you the basic steps for creating and producing a history Web site. It will also provide strategies for thinking critically about how Web sites may be used to convey solid historical research and information.

> Web projects allow you to build a narrative that interprets the past by weaving together images, documents, audiovisuals, graphic elements, and primary and secondary sources.

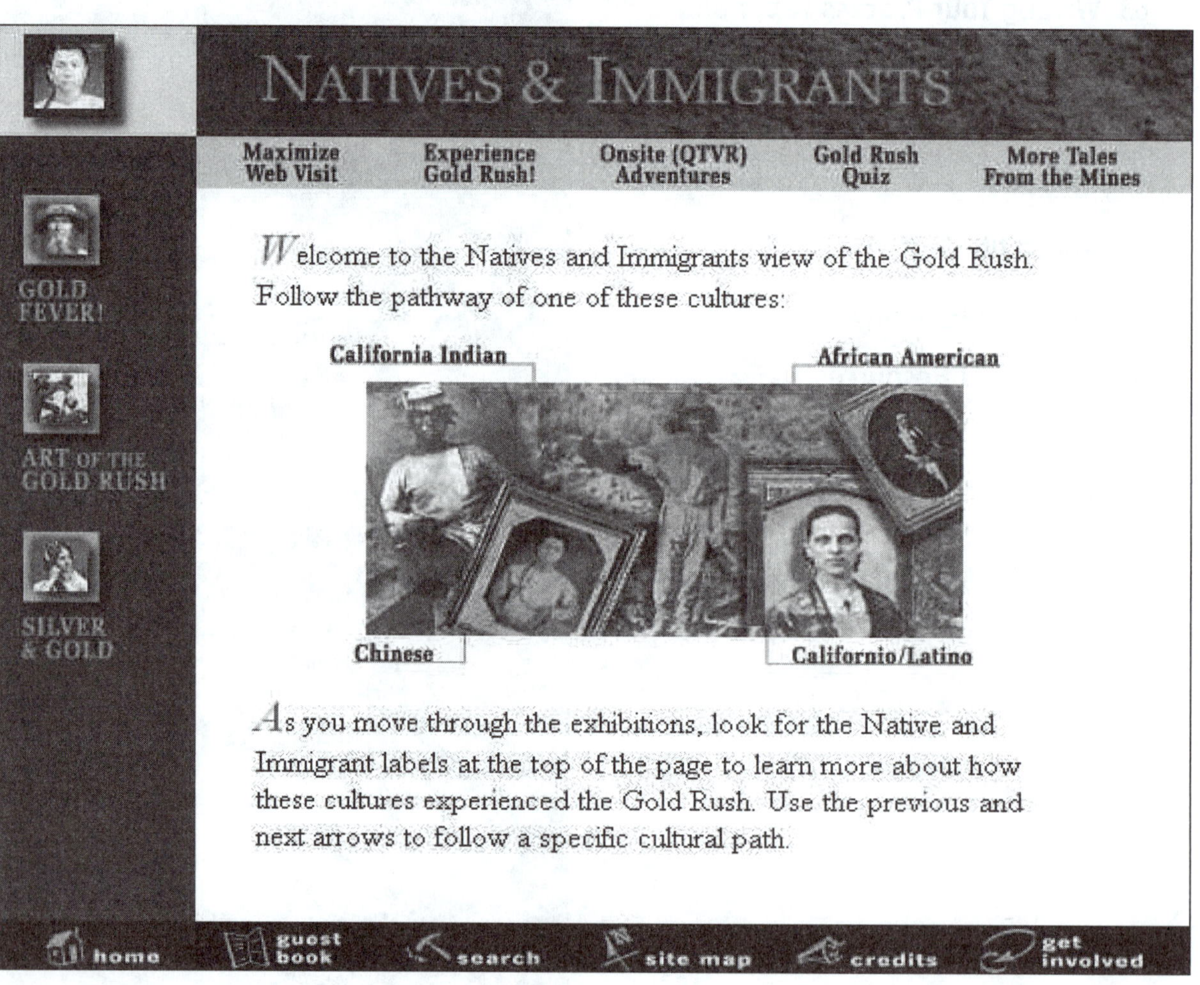

Notice the different perspectives presented on the Oakland Museum of California's Gold Rush Web site: California Indian, African American, Chinese, and Californio/Latino. View the site online and pay attention to the use of colors associated with the Gold Rush—gold and a complementary earthy burgundy.
http://www.museumca.org/goldrush/path.html

WHY A HISTORY WEB SITE?

A history Web site is a computer-based accumulation of research and argument that incorporates textual and nontextual description, interpretation, and multimedia sources to engage and inform viewers about historical topics. History Web sites present information and analyze events, people, places, and ideas from the past in dynamic online formats.

A good history Web site is more than just an electronic research paper or an online exhibit. On a Web site, you can link content, sources, and analysis. This format allows users to engage with your material through many different paths, exploring the questions they find most enticing at their own pace. You are also able to incorporate nontextual interactive elements, such as images, documents, maps, charts, time lines, music, interviews, videos, podcasts, and other media. At its core, though, your Web site should present sound historical analysis in addition to descriptive information.

Simply defined, a National History Day history Web site is an original collection of Web pages, interconnected with hyperlinks, that presents primary and secondary sources, interactive multimedia, and historical analysis.

WHY SHOULD I CONSIDER DOING A WEB SITE FOR NATIONAL HISTORY DAY?

The Web site category is great for students who enjoy working with computers and want to work with Web design software. Although many topics can be effectively conveyed using the Web site category, it is especially suitable for topics that have a variety of nontextual materials that can be used to support your argument.

This category requires additional equipment, so check the availability of the appropriate resources before you start. Do you have access to a computer with Web design software, either at home or at school? If you don't already know how to use the software program, is there someone at home or at school who can help you as you learn to use it? (Remember, people can help you with the software, but all the work in creating the Web site must be done by you individually or with your fellow group members.) Consider where you will have access to this equipment and where you will do most of your computer work. Discuss the answers to these questions with your parents and teachers.

Creating a Web site offers you many chances to work with technology. Whether you create your Web site using sophisticated computer software or free easy-to-use online programs, you will learn new skills because of the nature of the category. Working on a Web site gives you the opportunity to present some of the material you found during your research to a wide audience.

The Web site category might be a perfect fit if you:

- Enjoy working with design, programming, graphics, fonts, and color
- Have the skill and materials to build a Web site or an interest in learning how to build a Web site
- Want to practice writing clearly and concisely

> A good National History Day Web site emphasizes relationships among the raw materials of history. Your project should demonstrate those connections while constructing a historical narrative.

HOW ARE WEB SITES DIFFERENT FROM OTHER NATIONAL HISTORY DAY CATEGORIES?

You might think preparing a Web site is easier than writing a long paper, memorizing lines for a performance, making a documentary, or creating an exhibit. Building a Web site is fun, but it's also challenging. Your topic still needs to relate to the National History Day theme. You must have a clear, convincing thesis. You still need to do a lot of reading and research. You need to evaluate the evidence you find and select what you're going to display. And you need to make sure the elements of your design reflect your topic, whether it's your time period or your theme.

Creating a Web site is different from the other NHD categories in many ways:

- Web sites can display materials online—your own historical analysis as well as primary and secondary sources. These may include photographs, maps, and other images; written sources, such as diaries, letters, memoirs, or newspapers; and audio and video files and podcasts along with your analytical text.
- Web sites can be interactive experiences; viewers can play music, solve a puzzle, look at a video, or click on different links. The viewer becomes an active participant in your Web site, choosing how to engage with images, sound, video, and text.
- Web sites are hypertextual and nonlinear. Viewers can move through the different sections of the site in multiple, undirected ways.
- Web sites use color, images, fonts, documents, objects, graphics, and design, as well as words, to tell your story.
- NHD Web sites should not simply be an online text document or an archive of primary sources attached to an essay. You should provide historical analysis integrated with primary materials.

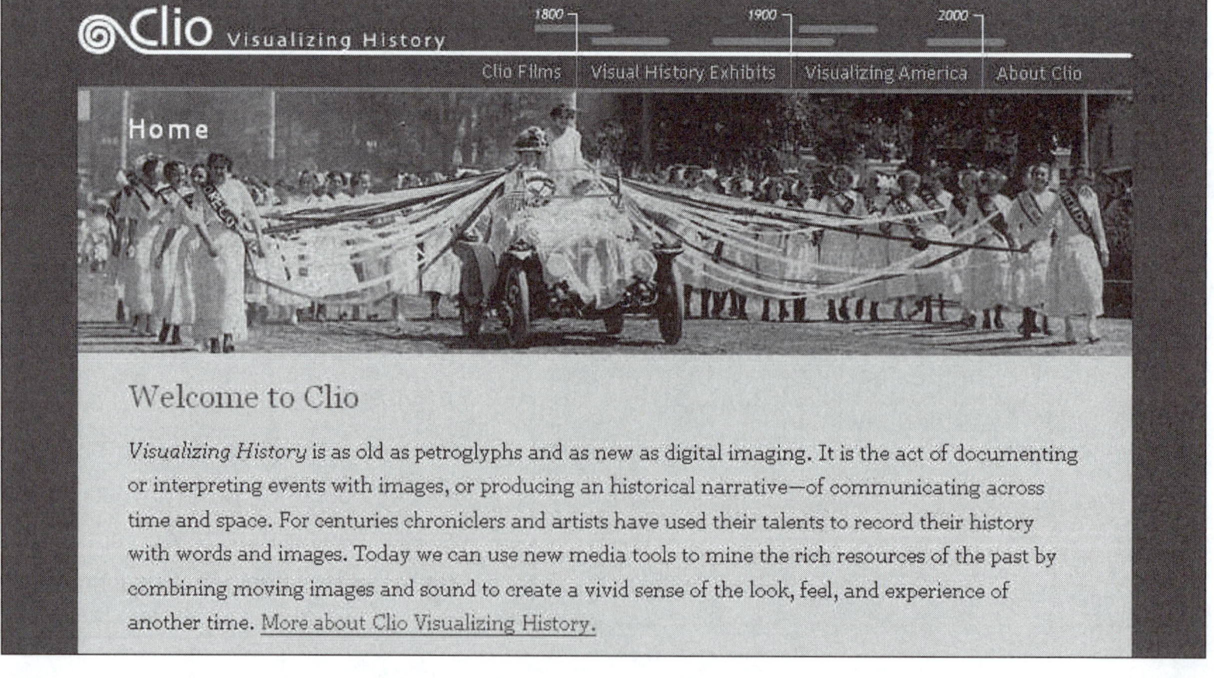

Clio Visualizing History uses a title, navigation bar, project purpose paragraph, image, and colors to contribute to its theme and tone. http://www.cliohistory.org/

BASIC NHD HISTORY WEB SITE FRAMEWORK

- ***Organization.*** Your Web site should include a home page with a menu directing the user to other pages. These pages do not need to be viewed sequentially. There should be a navigation system to guide users back and forth between the home page and the other pages.
- ***Browser.*** Your Web site must be viewable in a recent version of a standard Web browser (e.g., Microsoft Internet Explorer, Firefox, or Safari). Make sure your pages work in multiple browsers. The content and appearance of the site should not change when the page is refreshed in the browser. Random text or image generators are not allowed.
- ***Size limit.*** The overall size of your Web site can be no more than 100MB of file space, including all multimedia.
- ***Word limit.*** The Web site may contain no more than 1,200 visible, student-composed words. This means all words you write that are visible to the viewer count toward your word limit. If you didn't write it, it doesn't count toward the limit. Quotations from primary and secondary sources, such as oral history interviews, letters, diaries, newspaper articles, or photographs of articles with writing, will not count against your 1,200 words (just be sure every quote you use explicitly supports your thesis). Words that are not visible to the viewer, such as code used to build the site and alternate text tags on images, do not count against the word limit. Recurring text on menus and titles, as well as navigational words, are counted only once, not on each page where they appear. Brief text crediting the sources of illustrations and the annotated bibliography do not count toward your 1,200-word limit. The Web site's textual content must include historical analysis in your own words.

Examples of things that do count toward your word limit

- Headers, titles, subtitles, and navigational text—only counted once
- Graphs, charts, or time lines that you create yourself
- Captions with your analysis
- Words you write that appear on your Web pages

Examples of things that don't count toward your word limit

- Quotations
- Graphs, charts, or time lines that you don't create yourself
- Brief citations crediting the source of an illustration, quotation, or piece of media
- Code used to build the site and alternate text tags on images
- Transcriptions of primary documents
- Bibliography

IS A WEB SITE THE RIGHT CATEGORY FOR MY NATIONAL HISTORY DAY PROJECT?

If you believe you have good access to technology, people you can go to for help, and a desire to create a Web site, then this is the category for you. Keep in mind that not all topics will work well for the Web site category. If, for example, you pick a topic that has very few images, then a Web site may not be the best category for that topic. You can either change topics or change NHD categories if this is the case.

Before you decide to participate in this category, you should ask yourself the following questions:

- **Am I interested in using computers?**
- **Where will I have access to the equipment that will be needed to make a Web site (such as a computer, a scanner, and appropriate software)?**
- **What Web-design software program will I use?**
- **Who can assist me when I need help?**
- **What kinds of items will I display on my Web site?**
  - **Textual Documents:**
  - **Images:**
  - **Multimedia:**
- **What existing Web sites cover my topic?**
- **What makes my Web site different or unique?**
- **Is creating a Web site the best way to display my topic?**
  - **Why or why not?**
- **Would this topic be better as a paper, an exhibit, a documentary, or a performance?**

When you have answered these questions, it should be apparent whether or not you should create a NHD history Web site.

INDIVIDUAL VERSUS GROUP WORK

Most professional Web sites are built by teams, but for National History Day you can work solo or in a group. You should determine the pros and cons of either option and make the best decision for yourself.

- ***Individual.*** You are in control of every aspect of the research and design of your Web site. You alone will be responsible for the research, historical analysis, technical expertise, and design. You will have the flexibility and independence to develop your own creation.

- ***Group.*** You can draw on the expertise of other people in your group. It is very helpful to have everyone on the team discuss the thesis, content, and design. You will need to make sure everyone is on the same page and each member understands how to contribute. You will also need to assign specific responsibilities to each participant and be flexible enough to change assignments and help each other. Be aware that often in group work, certain people tend to pull more weight than others. Try to divide duties fairly and be accountable for your work.

- ***Time line.*** It may help to develop a time line for the project, whether you work individually or in a group. Set deadlines for each part of your project. In some cases, work by each team member can continue simultaneously. In others, one team member must complete a requirement before another team member can start or finish his or her assignments.

WHAT IS HISTORY?

All NHD projects involve learning about history, but often students are confused about just what "history" means.

History is more than what happened in the past. It is the *record* of past events, and it is *what historians write and present* about the past. NHD lets you become a historian and do what historians do. "Doing history" means not just finding documents and learning facts, but it's also a way of thinking and a set of skills.

Maybe you think history is about memorizing dates or reading dry textbooks or encyclopedia articles. Or maybe you think history is dull because it happened a long time ago and isn't important to us today. But history is much more exciting than that. Studying history tries to answer the question, "How did we get here?" History gets us to think about how past events shaped the present. Just as an individual needs to understand his or her family's past, its relationships, its problems, and its achievements, it is important for all of us to understand how societies began and changed and how people coped with the challenges of their time.

Studying history lets you step out of your time, social background, and place to examine how life was different from what it is today, and it helps you begin to understand people who are not like you. It gets you to think about what people believed and why they made the choices they made. Studying history exposes you to many human emotions: the lives of great men and women inspire us, as do the actions of ordinary individuals; accounts of injustices prompt us to anger; and stories of social and technological invention astonish us. Finally, history teaches important skills, such as reading carefully, collecting and evaluating evidence, drawing appropriate conclusions, thinking critically, and writing clearly.

The following list describes some of the skills and tools historians must develop and why you will need to use them in your project.

- ***Tell a story.*** To "do history" you have to tell a story. Your story will have a beginning, a middle, and an end, although through a Web site you may choose to present the story in a variety of ways. And like a spellbinding novel, your story will hold the reader's interest. Most importantly, your story will have a thesis, analysis, and conclusion. A skilled historian highlights some events as more important than others, and identifies and writes about dramatic incidents using colorful quotations, vivid images, and facts that bring the past to life. A Web site may not use as many words as a book, but it, too, needs to tell a story. Your Web site does not have to be linear; you might choose to organize it chronologically or thematically. Your visitors should be able to choose their own path through your story—rather than just hitting a "next" or "back" button—but your organization plan will help you to tell the history more clearly. And a good historical story includes sound analysis.

- ***Reveal change over time.*** It is easy to point out examples of changes in recent history. Teenagers no longer listen to their favorite bands on 45-rpm records; they download music from the Internet. Many more women work outside the home today than did so 50 years ago. Congress was recently controlled by the

Republicans and then by the Democrats. Historians are fascinated with change. They try to figure out not only how things changed (or didn't change), but why. As you work on your NHD Web site, don't just ask what happened, but inquire into what led to an event and why it happened at a specific moment in time, or why something may not have changed in an anticipated way. Be sure that your primary and secondary sources support your conclusions about why things happened the way they did.

- ***Consider historical perspective.*** Think about what you would tell someone about a day in the life of your school. You would probably describe what you did during the day, and maybe you would report on your friends' activities. But wouldn't you also want to include what your principal did? What about your teachers, the librarian, and the custodial staff? Wouldn't you want to include their stories and get their perspectives, too, so that you could create as complete a picture of the day as possible? Providing different perspectives will be important for your Web site.

When you investigate a historical event, it is also important to look for and understand the points of view of many participants—to look for *different historical perspectives* relating to your specific topic. For example, June 6, 1944—the day the Allies invaded Nazi-held Northern Europe—meant different things depending on who and where you were. An Allied infantryman on Omaha Beach had a very different perspective on the day than did General Dwight D. Eisenhower, the supreme commander of the invasion, who was in England. A French Resistance fighter had a different experience from that of a German soldier or an American woman working in an aircraft factory in California. A good historian considers these perspectives and weaves them into the story. A good Web site includes documents, images, and quotes that consider multiple perspectives, all pointing to a tight central analysis or argument.

- ***Provide context.*** Our lives are greatly influenced by when and where we live. People who lived in the past were equally shaped by their environment. A French peasant who lived in 1760 had only a few options about where he could live or work. A woman living in England in 1850 could not run for political office or even vote. Similarly, the places where people lived shaped how individuals and societies developed. The fact that Pope John Paul II was born in Poland profoundly affected the rest of his life. Communities and social institutions developed very differently in the dry American West than along New England's seashores.

Historians refer to an understanding of how time and place affect history as having an appreciation of *context.* A superior NHD Web site will illustrate how time and place influenced events. This can be done in a number of ways. A time line might note what other events happened at the same time as your topic. A letter or page of a memoir might describe how a person's hometown affected his or her outlook. A photo or image could be used to create an environment that reminds the viewer of the time and place in which a person lived. The colors used in a Web site could be the same as the flag of a nation or reflect the geography where an event took place.

One technique that may help you to think about the geographical context of an event is to ask "why there?" To think about how a time may have influenced an event ask, "why did something happen at this particular moment?"

- ***Ask questions.*** The stories a historian tells have a lot to do with the questions he or she asks about the past. Good questions come from a thorough understanding of your topic and the research you do. Sometimes these questions can't be answered by a simple yes or no. Instead, they will lead you to more questions. Important questions about the past result from thinking critically about your topic. Critical thinking does not mean disapproving or fault finding. Rather, it means analyzing what is important. Here are two examples of different types of historical questions—one easy and one more complex.

  1. Thomas Jefferson wrote the Declaration of Independence. Did he also own slaves? Yes. This is a simple yes or no question. It is based entirely on facts. Little discussion will flow from this question.

  2. Thomas Jefferson wrote the Declaration of Independence. He was also a slave owner. How did he reconcile his belief that "all men are created equal" with the fact that he was a slave owner? This is a much more complicated (and interesting!) question. To try to answer it, you need to know something about Jefferson's life and thought as well as the time in which he was living. This question also leads to many others. For example, how did Jefferson and men like him understand the meaning of the word "freedom"? What did Jefferson think about the question of equality between Europeans and African Americans? Did Jefferson think there were any alternatives except slavery and complete freedom for all slaves?

  Questions like these will also lead you to a variety of historical sources, such as biographies of Jefferson, his writings, and historical documents from the time.

- ***Draw conclusions.*** A good historian does more than just describe how events happened; he or she draws conclusions about the past. Your Web site needs to do this, too. Ideally, your conclusions will closely relate to the NHD theme. For example, if the NHD theme is "The Individual in History," a Web site about Martin Luther King Jr.'s philosophy of nonviolence might conclude that King's reading of Mahatma Gandhi was a key to the tactics he used in the civil rights movement. If the NHD theme is "Frontiers in History," your Web site on the space race could emphasize Cold War hostility and fear between the United States and the Soviet Union as the most important factor in the contest to get to the moon. As long as your conclusions are based on solid evidence, having a strong point of view or crafting an argument helps you create a good NHD Web site.

- ***Find facts, facts, and more facts.*** History is more than facts and dates, but that doesn't mean facts and dates aren't important to a historian. To tell a story, describe a time and place, ask questions of the past, and draw conclusions, you have to get your facts right. Being able to answer "who," "what," "when," and "where" about your topic will equip you to take on these more challenging tasks. Think of facts and dates as the foundation of a house you are constructing. Getting your facts right builds a solid foundation; inaccuracies will make the house fall down.

DESCRIPTIVE VERSUS INTERPRETIVE HISTORY

A good historian is a reporter, a detective, an analyst, a critic, and a philosopher. On the most basic level, you will arrange a report of events in chronological order, but you cannot simply describe the facts or restate what is in your history book. Records are often incomplete and contradictory, and without further commentary and discussion, a reporter-style history provides little analysis or sense of how the pieces fit together.

As a detective, the historian discovers facts by examining historical records. You can interpret the past by examining your topic in its proper historical context. What was going on in the neighborhood, town, country, or world? A good historian, like a detective, links the facts and comes to a well-documented conclusion. You should use descriptions gathered from your research of primary sources and secondary sources to interpret or find meaning from the tidbits of the past. Rather than merely describe history, your Web site should interpret or analyze history.

Another role is that of analyst or interpreter—to find meaning behind those facts. This often means making choices about the context and the meaning of historical events. You decide what is an important fact and why. As an analyst, you must sift through the evidence, present your findings, and decide what it all means. Remember that you will make choices about what is important and what isn't, using some facts and discarding others. Try to be open to all points of view.

When you act as a critic, you will offer assessment of the rights and wrongs of whatever happened in the past. You may also act as a philosopher, concentrating on ideas, questions, and attitudes surrounding your topic. The roles of analyst, critic, and philosopher may all work together in producing good interpretive history. You must synthesize, or bring together, a variety of ideas and evidence to forge them into a new pattern. You must give shape and coherence to the descriptive record. You may also become a storyteller, to an extent. You should present your information and your findings to show change over time, according to your specific thesis.

MAKING A HISTORICAL ARGUMENT

As you complete your research, you will search out facts on your topic. Making a historical argument requires you to first transform your facts into evidence, and then build your evidence into an argument. Be sure to select your evidence carefully—compare your sources, double-check your facts, be concerned about the biases of your records, and remember to stay strictly within the bounds of your thesis. Then you can make a strong argument.

A historical argument requires a strong thesis. One way to determine your thesis is to engage in questions. Start with a simple question:

Should the atomic bomb have been dropped on Japan?

By thinking more deeply, you can make your question a little more complex:

Given that the Japanese military establishment had vowed to fight to the bitter end, should the United States have dropped the bomb on Japan?

Given that the U.S. government was becoming increasingly concerned with postwar struggles with the Soviet Union, should the United States have dropped the bomb on Japan?

What impact did racism have on the decision to drop the bomb?

What impact did the brewing Cold War with the Soviet Union have on the decision to drop the bomb?

Soon your questions should lead to other questions, probing more deeply into the historical record:

Did racism lead the United States to drop the bomb on Japan? Would the United States have dropped an atomic bomb on Germany? How exactly did American views of the Japanese and Germans differ?

One simple question leads to a long chain of questions. Critical and analytical questions cannot be answered with "yes" or "no." Rather, they require a series of facts and provoke discussion that can be spread across your different Web pages.

Start with your topic:

Discrimination against Japanese Americans during World War II.

Develop your question:

Why did government officials allow and encourage discrimination against Japanese Americans?

Then develop a unique perspective for your historical argument:

Government officials allowed discrimination against Japanese Americans not because it was in the nation's interest, but because it provided a concrete enemy for people to focus on.

A historical argument involves critical questions, stemming from facts and interpretation.

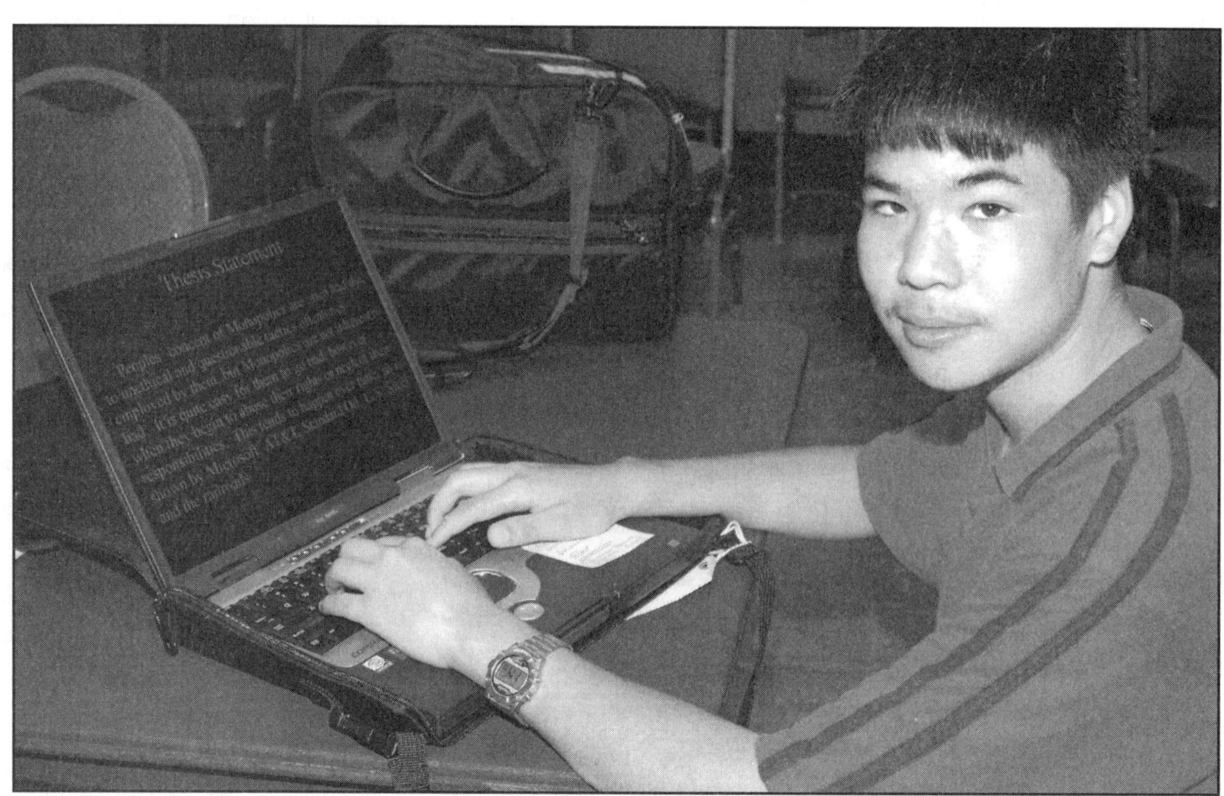

CHOOSING YOUR WEB SITE TOPIC

One of your first big decisions is to pick a topic for your NHD project. There is no one way to come up with a great topic. It might come from reading a book, discussing different ideas with a teacher or parent, watching a movie or a TV show, or surfing the Web. The following steps might help you to choose a topic that will work well for a Web site.

- ***Brainstorm topics that relate to this year's NHD theme.*** A good idea can pop up anywhere. One way to choose your topic is to select a commonly known story and then find a different angle that approaches the topic in a new way. There are also many unknown stories to tell. You might find a broad topic, such as the experiences of children during the Civil War, and see what resources are available. One key is to choose a topic that truly interests you, and remember to put it into historical context.

  NHD themes change each year. This year's theme may be "The Individual in History," and next year's theme might be "Innovation in History." Your topic needs to focus on the current year's theme. For example, if the theme is "Revolution, Reaction, Reform in History," you might consider topics such as the impact of the Solidarity labor movement on the fall of communism in Eastern Europe. If the theme is "Geography in History: Impact, Influence, Change," you might want to cover a topic such as the American West and its impact on immigration in the late 19th century or how and why cities developed along the Mississippi River. Or you might look at the way New York City's Broadway became the premier theater district in the country. Remember, *relation to the theme* counts for 20 percent of the score you receive from the contest judges, so look for a topic that will match the theme closely.

  Keeping in mind this year's NHD theme, flip through history textbooks, browse the Internet, or talk to family members and teachers for good historical topics. Download and complete the NHD Topic Selection Worksheet from the NHD Web site http://www.nhd.org/CreatingaProject.htm to help you select your topic.

The National History Day theme for 2007—
Triumph & Tragedy in History

The National History Day theme for 2008—
Conflict & Compromise in History

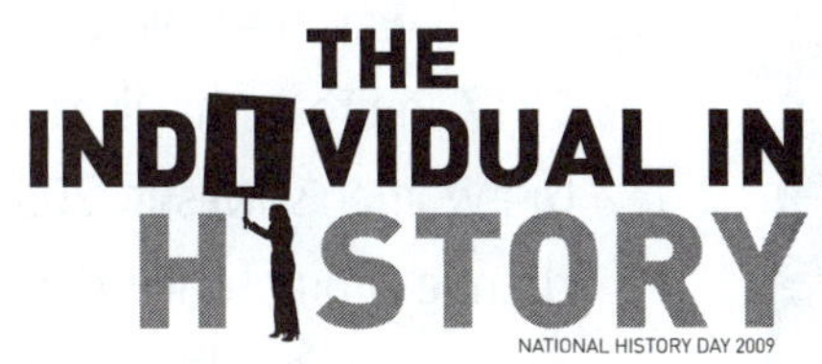

The National History Day theme for 2009—
The Individual in History: Actions and Legacies

- ***Determine what historical resources are nearby.*** You don't have to travel to China to do your research on building the Great Wall, and you don't have to go to Johannesburg to study the antiapartheid movement. You can obtain primary research materials from local libraries, from the Internet, and from interviews with participants who live near you. If you have a passionate interest in a topic, go for it! Your enthusiasm and research can make up for your lack of nearby sources.

  Choosing a topic for which a number of primary sources are available in your region has its advantages, however. A local historical society may have diaries or letters from participants in a historical event. A regional archive may have photographs, film, or sound recordings that relate to your topic. Newspaper accounts may be available on microfilm at a nearby library or college.

- ***Think through controversial topics.*** What led President Truman to order American airmen to drop the first atomic bomb on Japan? What limitations have governments put on free speech during wartime? Did the Bolshevik Revolution of 1917 improve the lives of the Russian people? Did women's lives in 20th-century United States change dramatically during World War II or did change take place more gradually over the course of the century? Historians and Web site designers deal with controversial subjects such as these all the time. Lively debates among historians about sensitive topics are part of what makes history so fascinating, and many thoughtful points of view can be found on most historical subjects. If you are thinking about tackling a controversial historical issue, be sure to discuss it first with a parent or guardian and your teacher. Of course, your topic will need to relate to the NHD theme. Most importantly, your NHD project needs to deal with the topic *in history*. If, for example, you are going to prepare a Web site about the Second Amendment to the Constitution and "the right to bear arms," remember that your exhibit should focus on the history of the amendment. It is *not* an opportunity to give your opinion on current gun-control controversies.

- ***Examine other history Web sites on your topic.*** Look at Web sites with similar ideas. How do these compare to what you want to do? Can you use some of their ideas in your own way? How can you provide a fresh, unique approach? What do you like or not like about these Web sites? What kinds of problems do they have with their account of history? With their navigation? With their presentation of images and information? What is missing?

Just as important as following the NHD theme is selecting a topic you find interesting. You are going to be working on your project for several months; picking a topic that interests you will make that time much more enjoyable.

CHOOSING YOUR WEB SITE TOPIC AND THESIS

- What is your topic?
- What is your thesis? What is your argument or angle with this topic?
- How does your topic illustrate this year's National History Day theme?
- What are your main points? What will you illustrate on your various Web pages as aspects of your main thesis?
- How can you narrow your topic?
- How will you explore and present your topic with primary sources?
- What multimedia forms will you use?
- How will your viewers engage with your Web site?
- What kind of balanced context will you provide?

CONDUCTING HISTORICAL RESEARCH

WEB SITE

Do Your Secondary Research First

You've chosen a great topic. Your teacher has approved it, and you can't wait to visit a local archive, interview someone who participated in the historical event, or read old newspaper stories about it.

Stop!

Every historian looks forward to doing research by diving into the *primary sources.* If you are excited about history, it's only natural to want to read a letter from the 18th century, listen to an early sound recording, or hold an old map in your hands. But before you start looking for those primary sources, you need to prepare by first reading *secondary sources*—books and journal articles written by historians on your topic—talking with experts, and visiting trustworthy Web sites that will give you accurate information. These steps will help you understand your subject more completely, point you toward primary sources, and select the important themes you want to investigate and the key questions you want to ask.

Encyclopedias and online sources can provide helpful overview information, are useful for looking up facts, and will sometimes lead you to additional resources. Because encyclopedias do not include an interpretation of these facts, you should not rely heavily on these sources. Use them to get a better idea of the broader topic, time period, and context, as well as the basic dates and events, and then turn to more detailed sources, such as books and journal articles written specifically on your topic.

Secondary sources, such as scholarly articles or books, are most easily found in libraries. A good place to find secondary sources is on the Web. When they are available online, they are often accessible only through fee-based subscriptions. Sometimes these are accessible at your school library. See http://www.nhd.org/images/uploads/AResearchRoadmap.pdf for additional ideas on good secondary sources.

A NOTE ABOUT wikipedia.org

wikipedia.org is a collectively authored online encyclopedia, meaning that anyone can edit entries at any time. As a rule, wikipedia summarizes and reports conventional and accepted wisdom on a topic, but, similar to other encyclopedias, does not include original research or interpretation of facts. wikipedia receives mixed reviews.

Critics charge that the online encyclopedia is inaccurate because entries can be written and edited by virtually anybody—experts and nonexperts—and that the information is biased. There is not a given single author for any entry. Supporters claim that because multiple authors collectively produce information about topics, there is a greater likelihood that someone will catch and correct errors. Another issue with wikipedia is that entries constantly change, making it difficult to track information. Like any other online resource, wikipedia can provide basic ideas about a topic but facts should be evaluated in the same way you evaluate other online information. Compare information from several sources and assess the accuracy of each.

Evaluating Secondary Sources

When working with primary and secondary sources, it is important to remember that history is not a simple, fixed narrative. Historians debate, discuss, and even disagree about the various sources and interpretations of the past. Many factors shape historical events and historians also look at how things might have happened given different circumstances or when seen through another pair of eyes. For example, our understanding of history changes when we look at the experiences of political leaders versus the daily lives of those who were not known nationally or internationally. Looking at multiple perspectives can provide a more complex understanding of the past. Equally important is the skill of investigating the past carefully and with an open mind, allowing yourself to see things that may not fit with the larger narrative you have learned. Keep your mind open and examine several different sources.

As you read through your secondary sources, you will discover that authors and even professional historians bring their own biases to the topics they research. You should learn to recognize their opinions, what they believe is most important, and what they leave out. You should also learn that there are differences in the quality of information about your historical topic. The following guidelines will help you as you evaluate the authenticity of your secondary sources.

- ***Pay attention to the intended audience.*** Popular books (e.g., Tom Brokaw's *The Greatest Generation*) and magazines (e.g., *National Geographic, American History Illustrated, Civil War Times*) are usually written for a general audience, while researchers and scholars read monographs (full-length books dealing

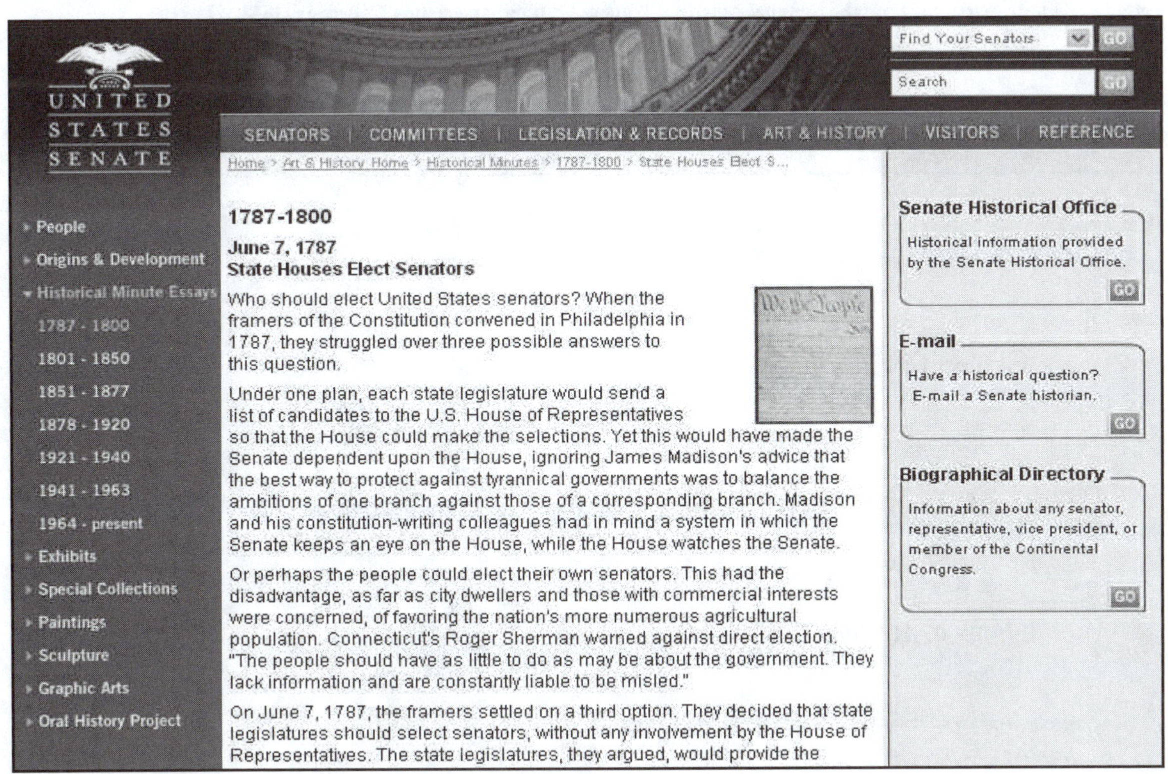

The United States Senate presents several essays as secondary sources. Notice the thumbnail of the Constitution, where viewers can go for more detailed information as a primary source.
http://www.senate.gov/artandhistory/history/minute/State_Houses_Elect_Senators.htm

with a relatively narrow topic, like Laurel Thatcher Ulrich's *A Midwife's Tale: The Life of Martha Ballard, Based on Her Diary, 1785–1812*) and academic journals (e.g., *American Historical Review, Journal of American History, William & Mary Quarterly*). Although popular books and magazines may provide high-quality illustrations and provocative, conversational reading, academic writing will provide more authoritative information.

- ***Look for documentation—sources and footnotes.*** Good footnotes will likely lead you to other sources, including some you may not have anticipated. Lack of documentation makes it difficult to evaluate the quality and authenticity of information. Without source information, it is difficult to figure out how the author came up with his or her conclusions.

- ***Check dates of publication.*** You should use the most up-to-date writing about your topic because ideas change as new information is made available.

- ***Take account of the publisher.*** Although general publishers like Alfred Knopf produce solid academic work, university presses publish the majority of scholarly work.

The Exciting World of Primary Sources

NHD defines primary sources as *materials related to a topic by time or participation.* These primary sources

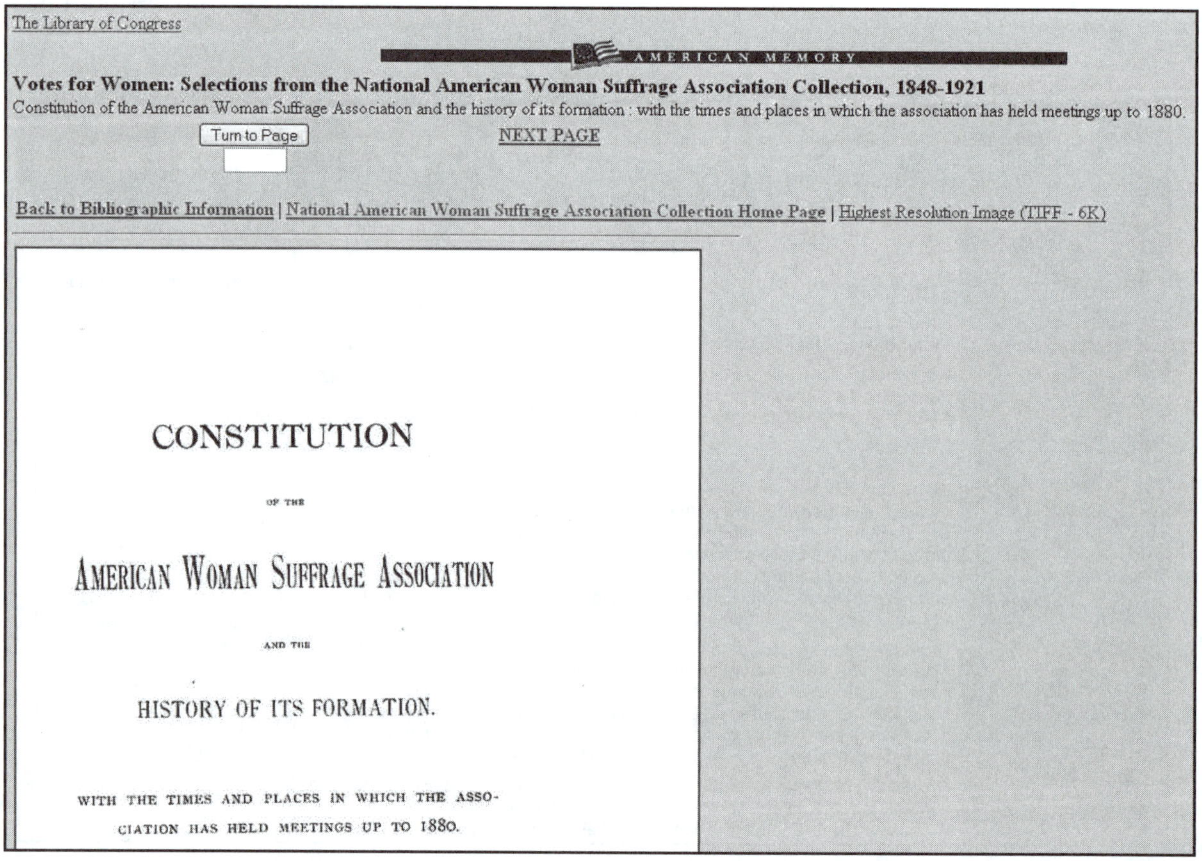

The Library of Congress

AMERICAN MEMORY

Votes for Women: Selections from the National American Woman Suffrage Association Collection, 1848-1921
Constitution of the American Woman Suffrage Association and the history of its formation : with the times and places in which the association has held meetings up to 1880.

Turn to Page

NEXT PAGE

Back to Bibliographic Information | National American Woman Suffrage Association Collection Home Page | Highest Resolution Image (TIFF - 6K)

CONSTITUTION

OF THE

AMERICAN WOMAN SUFFRAGE ASSOCIATION

AND THE

HISTORY OF ITS FORMATION.

WITH THE TIMES AND PLACES IN WHICH THE ASSOCIATION HAS HELD MEETINGS UP TO 1880.

The Library of Congress Web site contains countless primary sources, such as an online version of the Constitution of the National Woman's Suffrage Association. http://hdl.loc.gov/loc.rbc/rbnawsa.n8291

might take the form of letters or diaries, manuscript collections, photographs, drawings and other works of art, songs, maps, government records, newspapers, magazines, oral history interviews, or artifacts. See http://www.nhd.org/images/uploads/AResearchRoadmap.pdf for more detailed information about primary sources. As you examine primary sources in your research, you may want to consider including some on your Web site.

Sorting out primary from secondary sources can be complicated. The key to spotting a primary source is the phrase, *by time or participation.* For example, a newspaper article from 1878 describing that year's Paris International Exposition is a primary source. If the article was written by a journalist who visited the Exposition or an architect who designed one of the buildings, it is also connected to the event through participation. An article or book about the Exposition written in 2001 by a historian is a secondary source.

Other types of primary sources need to be evaluated by using the same test. A taped interview with a historian about prisoners of war during World War II is a secondary source unless that historian was also a prisoner or participated in some other way—for example, if he was a soldier who helped to liberate the prison. A song sung by British troops in the trenches during World War I is a primary source from the World War I era. A song written by a songwriter looking back on the war from today could tell us about perceptions of the war in the 21st century, but it would not tell us how people experienced the war in the early 20th century. Sometimes the same source can be both primary and secondary, depending on how it is being used. A history textbook is usually a secondary source, but what if you were doing an exhibit about how American history textbooks in the 1950s discussed the causes of the Civil War? Then, a textbook published in 1954 would become a primary source.

Hundreds, or even millions, of primary sources are available on almost any subject in world history. Think about what kinds of sources are most relevant to your project and then start with background research. Are there just a few resources available? Can you review them all? Do you need to narrow your topic?

Now that you understand the definition of primary sources, how do you find them? A good first step is to look at the secondary source books and articles you read. They will often have footnotes and bibliographies that refer you to manuscript collections, oral histories, photography holdings, and other sources. Another approach is to talk with your librarian or teacher and get their suggestions. Or you might want to contact a university professor who specializes in your subject area, and ask what primary sources are available for your subject. Vast quantities of primary sources, such as diaries, films, and manuscript collections, are not available digitally and may never be. You may need to dig through sources at local or regional archives, libraries, historical societies, and special collections. Many archives have extensive online search aids that will help you determine if their collections have something that would help you. See the Finding Primary Sources Online section on page 24 for more ideas.

Evaluate Your Primary Source Evidence

Learning various research strategies to analyze historical evidence creates new opportunities and introduces new questions. When you think carefully about the kinds of materials you are using and what they tell you that other resources cannot, your research question will become more refined and you may be led to unexpected conclusions. Start by asking general questions, move to specific questions relevant for that source, and then explore how the primary source fits into a larger context.

Just because a source was created at the time of the event you are studying or by a participant in that event doesn't mean it's true or more important than other sources. The primary sources you display are evidence and, thus, need to be evaluated, analyzed, and interpreted. This process will allow you to judge how valuable each source is to the story you are telling and to the points you are trying to make. Here are some important questions to ask about any source.

- ***What type of source is this?*** Evaluating different types of sources calls for different sets of skills and raises new questions. You may be able to read a letter easily for the information it contains (unless it is in a foreign language or has handwriting difficult to read). "Reading" a poster requires knowledge of the life of the artist, the techniques he or she used to create it, the symbolism it contains, and its intended audience. Knowing something about the type of source will also help you to think about the past in different ways. A photograph of the civil rights march in Selma, Alabama, for example, may raise a different set of questions for you than would a written description of the march.
- ***What is the date of the source?*** When and where was it created? What happened after its first appearance? How did the source survive? Why is it available in the 21st century? Dating a document allows you to put it into historical perspective—to place it in time. A petition about the U.S. military draft written just before World War II will have a very different historical context than one written during the Vietnam War. A date can also tell you something about the reliability of the source. A diary entry from the day an event happened offers a different perspective than a memoir written 50 years later, even if both were written by the same participant.
- ***Who created this source?*** What do you know about that person or group of people? What do you know about an author's motives, intentions, or point of view? Is the creator in a position to be a good reporter? Why or why not? If you know who created a primary source, you can learn something about why it was created and for what purpose. Newspaper accounts are usually factual but may be biased by the paper's political views. A letter written by someone involved in a scandal may try to justify his or her actions. A photograph of children working in a coal mine may have been taken by someone who wants to pass legislation to end child labor. Learning about the motivation of the creator will help you analyze the source.
- ***Where was the source produced?*** This question raises issues of historical context. Two sources documenting the same event that were created in two different places may have dramatically dissimilar views of that event. A newspaper account of the Confederate attack on Fort Sumter in 1861 written in Boston, Massachusetts, would likely differ from one written in Charleston, South Carolina, much as an oral history from a Russian would be different from that of a Cuban talking about the Cuban Missile Crisis.

- ***What can you learn from the source?*** Start by carefully reading or analyzing the source. For a written document, consider the kind of source, tone, and word choice. Pay attention to parts of speech—what kinds of nouns or adjectives are used? Does this remain consistent throughout the document or does it change? How formal or informal is the language? Is the account believable? Is it internally consistent or are there contradictions? For an image, look carefully at each section separately and then look at the whole. Listen to a song or watch a video multiple times. What does the source say or look like or sound like? What might it mean? What does each section mean? How do the sections work together? What questions come up as you carefully analyze the source itself?

- ***What about the context of the source?*** Consider the larger historical picture and situate the source within a framework of events and perspectives, paying close attention to *when* they happened and *where* they took place. When was the source created? What else was happening at this time that may have influenced its creation? How might an intended or unintended audience have shaped the source? How might location have influenced its creation? Looking at multiple perspectives can provide a more complex understanding of the past. In addition, learning to understand the past, to connect it to a larger story, is key.

- ***Does the source check out with other sources?*** Whenever possible, corroborate important details against other sources. Evaluate multiple sources in relationship to one another, and look for similarities and contradictions. Look at key content and stylistic differences. Where do the sources agree with one another? Where do they disagree? What viewpoint does each source reflect? Which sources seem more reliable or trustworthy? Why? Which would be the better primary source for you to use or include on your Web site or would it be more interesting to present both for comparison?

Primary sources are "the raw stuff of history," and they will be an important part of your Web site research. However, don't forget that to get the most out of your sources, you need to have a thorough knowledge of your topic based on your reading in secondary sources. As you study your primary sources, reread some of the secondary accounts. You may find you have new insights or realize you have new questions to ask. You may need to find more secondary sources.

RESEARCH ON THE WEB

The World Wide Web has made conducting historical research much easier and has placed huge numbers of historical documents at your fingertips. Browsing is very helpful when you are starting a project and do not have a specific resource or topic in mind. A well-designed Web site allows you to wander around thematic or chronological sections and to see connections and groupings. Many reputable universities, libraries, museums, archives, government agencies, and other organizations have accurate and reliable Web sites.

A simple Google search may turn up countless Web sites on your topic, without any indication as to how credible a site may be. Some kinds of materials are more readily available online than others. It is relatively easy to find online photographs, newspapers, and personal accounts for studying U.S. history; it is more challenging to find archaeological information, music, or quantitative evidence. It is important, therefore, to know how to find good, solid history on the Internet.

Most Web sites contain secondary source content. This may include explanatory or contextualizing text that introduces the topic or explains a particular source or leads to a bibliography of related scholarly articles and books. These secondary source materials provide both a context for understanding the sources and an entry point into the conversation that historians are having about a particular topic.

- ***Don't try to do all your research on the Web.*** Information on the Web tends to simplify complicated issues. Remember, too, that *anyone* with a little skill with Web site design can put *anything* they want on a site, no matter how inaccurate. Some sites are also associated with groups that have financial, political, religious, or other motives for presenting information from a specific perspective. They may choose to cite "facts" that agree with their point of view and not mention those that don't fit in with the cause they are promoting.

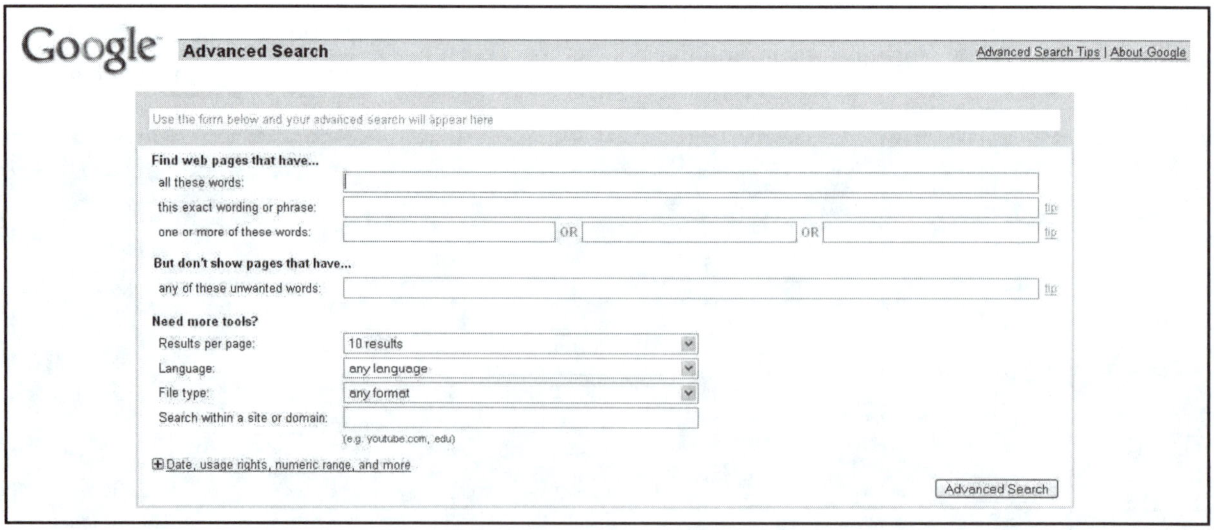

Google Advanced Search — Advanced Search Tips | About Google

Use the form below and your advanced search will appear here

Find web pages that have...
all these words:
this exact wording or phrase: tip
one or more of these words: OR OR tip

But don't show pages that have...
any of these unwanted words: tip

Need more tools?
Results per page: 10 results
Language: any language
File type: any format
Search within a site or domain: (e.g. youtube.com, .edu)

Date, usage rights, numeric range, and more

Advanced Search

Using an advanced Google search will give you more control over the results. You can select search terms, file types, or topic-specific search engines. http://www.google.com/advanced_search?hl=en

TIPS FOR SUCCESSFUL WEB SEARCHES

- ***Use quotation marks and use multiple terms to make your search more specific.*** If you enter the words "U.S. history," without quotes, Google returns more than 130 million results. If you put the search term in quotes ("U.S. history") you narrow it down to six million. Entering the specific topic, time period, or region you are interested in exploring, such as "U.S. history" and "Scopes Trial," will narrow it still further.

- ***Use Google's Advanced Search feature.*** This allows you to narrow your search to specific languages, include or exclude words or phrases, restrict domain names (.edu, .org, or .gov as more credible sources), or define the location of occurrences (e.g., the phrase occurs anywhere on the page, only in the title, or only in the text of a Web page).

- ***Use the + : – | and ~ signs to increase the accuracy of your search results.*** The minus sign (–) means *not*, the solid vertical line (|) substitutes for *or*, and the (~) suggests a synonym. If you are searching for information on the John Scopes trial, you might try *John Scopes | monkey + trial* because the trial was also called the "Monkey Trial." Or, if you wanted search results that excluded wikipedia, you would use *John Scopes | monkey – wikipedia* to access more carefully selected search results. If you are not sure about different names for the same thing, try using (~) to include synonyms of that term.

Finding Primary Sources Online

Primary sources provide the opportunity to engage directly with the past, to try to sort out what happened and why. One of the strengths of the Web site category is that you can link your primary sources to your historical analysis. Digital primary sources include photographs, prints, paintings, government documents, advertisements, religious emblems, musical recordings, speeches, films, letters, newspaper articles, sermons, and material culture such as pottery, furniture, or tools. Chances are good that a simple Google search will not return many primary sources. A custom Google search, like the one found at teachinghistory.org/history-content, searches on reviewed Web sites, including the Library of Congress, the National Archives, the Gilder Lehrman Collection, and other repositories, many of which offer digitized primary documents.

Remember that the Web site may be a portal to primary sources at a local repository. Not all primary documents are online. You may need to physically visit a historical society, an archive, or a museum to use their information.

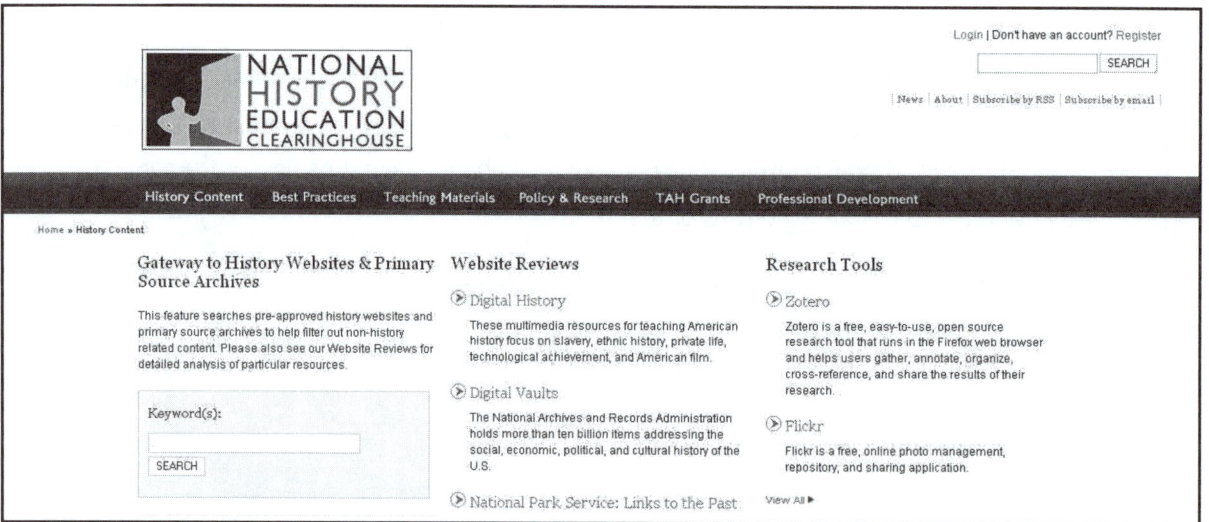

The National History Education Clearinghouse Web site includes a very helpful search engine for primary sources from reputable Web sites. http://teachinghistory.org/history-content

EVALUATING WEB SITES

Although Web sites can offer valuable material previously unavailable to many students, those related to history can also be the purveyors of misinformation, poorly translated texts, or biased narratives. Online history is also uneven in terms of regional and chronological coverage. So how do you wade through this enormous and sometimes confusing online world to find reliable information and resources? How can you avoid advertisements or personal pages with questionable standards of historical analysis? The key is finding quality materials that relate to your specific theme or topic. Part of doing online research means you must evaluate whether a Web site is a good, authoritative source or not. The most important way to become an intelligent consumer of historical resources online is to become a good historian by learning to use and apply the skills of critical analysis that historians rely on. Here are some guidelines that can help you figure out the reliability of a particular Web site.

- ***Credibility of the creator.*** Check the URL. If this is a personal Web site, you will need to check the authority of the author. The domain name (.com, .org, .gov, .edu) can also tell you more about the site. If there is a strong institution attached to the Web site, like the Library of Congress or a university, the site is more credible than if there is no institution. Is the author credible? Look for an "About Us," "Biography," or "Background" link and determine the author's credibility. Does the creator have the experience and research background to produce authoritative information? A good researcher will approach all Web sites with skepticism and will ask questions about why this material is available and who funded and created the Web site. As a rule of thumb, though, Web sites created by museums, libraries, and colleges are designed to present historical resources for educational purposes. Personal Web sites are often created to share an individual's passion for a certain topic and may or may not offer credible content. If the origin of the Web site is questionable, you probably shouldn't use it—or you should check the information against other sources.

- ***Point of view.*** An openly biased Web site can still provide useful information, but it is most valuable when it clearly identifies its goals and distinguishes between fact and opinion. Is there a clear presentation or selection of materials? Is the Web site selling something? One last question is whether the creators of the Web site have a particular ideological, religious, or analytical agenda and how that agenda might shape the selection of resources. A good Web site will present several options or explanations to an argument. As a general rule, controversial topics require extra investigation and a very careful reading of the contextual material on the Web site. Be especially skeptical if (a) a topic is very controversial; (b) you cannot determine who the author is; and (c) you find obvious biases. Point of view can also affect online collections of primary sources as someone strongly committed to one interpretation of the past might select primary sources that largely support that position. A good researcher will try to determine the author's point of view and then evaluate how that perspective might affect the interpretation of sources presented. If the Web site is selling something, the information it provides may not be entirely objective. You may have to check the information against other sources.

- ***Web sources.*** A good Web site will provide full citations for its information. Some Web sites may include excerpts instead of the full source. This may or may not make a difference in your research, but be aware of how complete your sources are. Some Web sites may not provide citations on the original sources, making it difficult to be sure the sources are authentic. Have the sources been altered in any way? Does the text appear to be complete or an excerpt? When looking at an image, it is hard to determine if something is an original or has been cropped or changed. Image-editing tools make alterations simple, and edited photographs can look very authentic. First, check to see if the creators discuss this issue anywhere on the Web site. Second, ask yourself if anything about the image might suggest that it has been altered. Do the colors seem unnatural? Have you seen other versions of this image that included features or people not in the current one? Similar questions hold true for video and audio sources, especially with the increasing popularity of online media and the capability of creating alternate versions of well-known sources. Does an audio or video clip seem edited or incomplete? Are there unnatural moments or cuts that might indicate editing or deletions? Might this be a spoof? If anything in the source gives you pause, look for a more complete version.

- ***Double-check information.*** Be careful about where links take you. Sometimes a link can take you to an entirely different site and you will need to check its credentials as well. An additional way to assess the reliability of a Web site is to investigate its reputation. Which other Web sites and organizations find it valuable?

Run a "link check" with Google by typing "link" and the complete URL into the Google search field. Results will list Web sites that include this one as a credible link and can provide telling information about how other people view this Web site. Considering all of these factors will help give you a good sense of the quality of a Web site and the materials it presents.

- ***Date.*** Information about when a Web site was created or updated can also be a valuable indicator of a Web site's reliability, although an archive of primary sources need not be updated frequently to remain useful. Web sites generally display the date of their most recent update. Remember, though, that just because a date is current doesn't mean all the information on the site has been updated. An old date, however, can clue you in that the site hasn't been updated in a while. Perhaps more current information is available. Older Web sites that are not maintained generally have problems such as broken links. Currency may also matter because recent research can shed new light on historical questions or translations.

- ***Audience.*** Information will be presented differently for children, teens, college students, academics, and the general public. What difference does the audience make for this Web site? Like the difference between popular books and magazines and scholarly monographs and journals, knowing the intended audience gives you a better idea of how credible the information is.

NHD has created an excellent Web site about evaluating Internet sites. For this and other research tips, go to http://www.nationalhistoryday.org/ResearchSources.htm.

USING QUOTATIONS

When using quotations, either from primary or secondary sources, it is your job to make it clear to the judges that these are not your own words by using quotation marks and by carefully labeling each source with its bibliographic information. This includes core information about the source, for example, identifying a letter from Thomas Jefferson to the president pro tempore of the Senate on March 2, 1801, as well as information on where you found the source, in this case on an American Memory Web site on presidential inaugurations. Including other people's work under the impression that it's yours is plagiarism.

- Who created the Web site? Who selected the sources presented there? How are they presented? Who is providing the financial support for the project?

- What are the aims of the Web site? Is there a particular slant? Is the information objective or subjective? Is the information biased in any way? Does it present a balanced opinion? Content can also be revealing. Does it present facts or opinions? Does it have a particular bias or point of view?

- Where do the sources on the Web site come from?

- Can the information presented on the Web site be confirmed by another Web site or by books? Are there links to other sites? Who else considers this a good Web site?

- When was the Web site created? Has it been updated recently?

- Who is the intended audience?

As you search on the internet, you may want to start collecting items in a folder for potential use. There are several different ways to copy images and documents from Web sites. You can right (control)-click and save the image into your own file, for instance. Make sure you are taking the image from a credible source, and make sure it is a quality image. Remember that you have size limits for your total site, but it is easier to save an image at a higher quality and then make it smaller than it is to try to make a poor image into one of a better quality. Keep track of where you find everything.

ZOTERO

As you come across primary sources that you may want to include on your Web site, carefully take notes on what you found and where you found it for your bibliography. One helpful way to collect, manage, and cite your research sources is with Zotero, a free extension for use with Firefox. This program allows for automatic capture of citation information from Web pages, flexible note taking, playlist-like library organization, and storage of PDFs, files, images, links, and whole Web pages. Zotero can be downloaded at http://www.zotero.org.

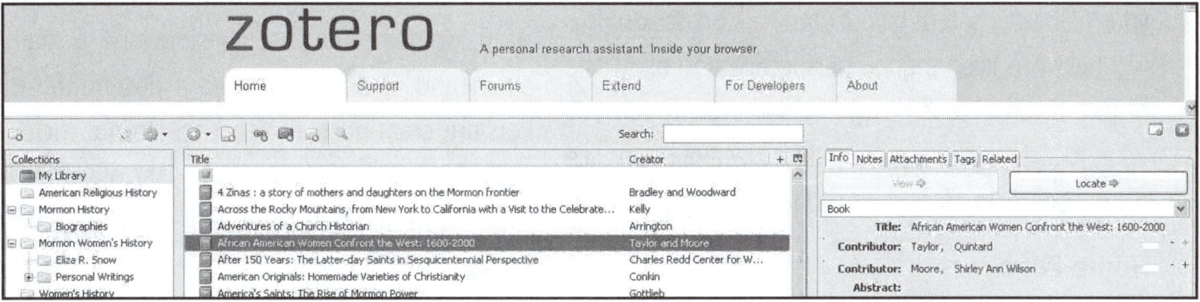

Zotero is a free program that helps students and teachers collect, manage, and cite research sources. http://www.zotero.org

HISTORY WEB SITE CONTENT

Web sites present many exciting opportunities to use design skills and to display graphics and multimedia items. It is important to remember that the National History Day guidelines specify that 60 percent of the judge's critique of your Web site is based on historical quality. You must communicate a strong central thesis, provide authentic historical context, and present wide, balanced research. Thus, it is a good idea to determine your Web site content before you work on design. This will help you keep a good perspective and allow the history to drive your design. At some point you will want to sketch your ideas out on a piece of paper, like a story board. But first you need to have solid content.

Home Page

Consider your home page like the introduction of a paper. Your home page is the first opportunity to present who you are and what your site is all about. You do not need an introductory page that asks your viewer to click to enter your home page; instead, bring your visitors immediately into your Web site. The home page is a great place to introduce your project. Let your viewer know right away the argument you will be making. Set the tone for your Web site visually with appropriate graphics, colors, and text to match your topic and time period.

Your home page must include the names of the participants, entry title, division, and a main Web site menu. It does not need a description of why you are creating the Web site. Do not include the name of your school or your city or state. It is a good idea to include a link to your annotated bibliography in your navigation bar. Save your home page with the file name "index."

Just as every good paper has a strong thesis, so every good NHD history Web site should have a thesis. As you lay out your different arguments and the pages making up your site, you may want to include a

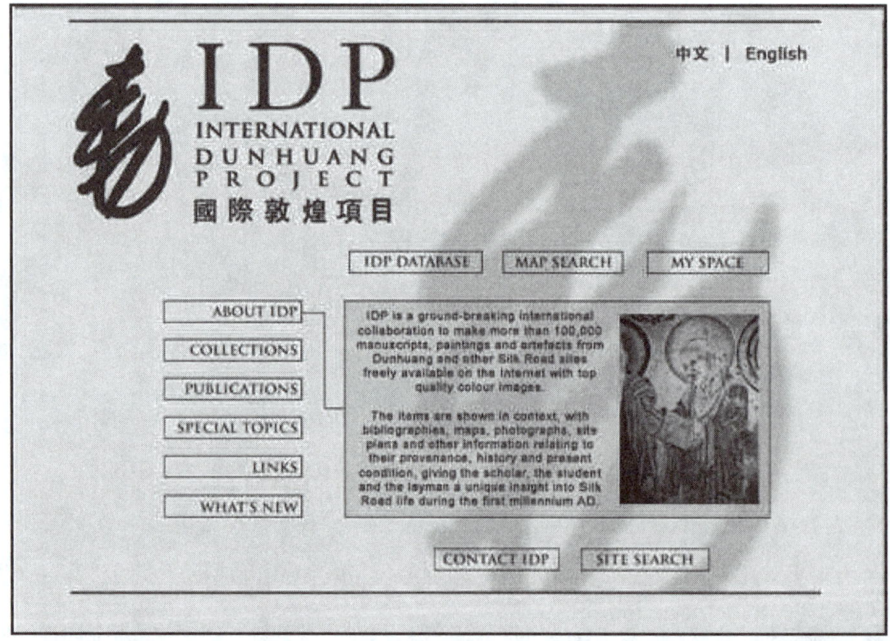

An early version of the British Library's International Dunhuang Project's home page clearly lays out a summary of the site. Rollovers on each link provide detailed information. This site is no longer available, but the page can be viewed at http://chnm.gmu.edu/digitalhistory/exploring/3.php, in Digital History: A Guide to Gathering, Preserving, and Presenting the Past on the Web

sentence or two about interior pages, sort of like a preview on your home page. Your home page is also a great location to present your thesis: What is your main idea? How will the different pages on your site illustrate this idea? Make sure your thesis is clearly presented on your home page. Remember to be brief: each word counts.

Similar to the process of writing a paper, sometimes it's difficult to start with the introduction, or your home page. You may need to put off making your home page until the rest of your content and design has been determined.

Argument

Every good history project has a strong thesis and a clear argument to support and defend that thesis. An argument is a set of propositions that provide persuasive evidence for why your thesis is true. The argument is not just an opinion, but proof. You should base your argument on a solid understanding of the issues and the evidence you discovered in your research.

Your argument may be visibly divided by the different pages on your Web site. Just as you would for a paper, think about the main points. Decide what you have to say—how you have interpreted the historical facts—for each point. This text will be the core of your argument, and the majority of the text on your Web site. You'll also need to decide which primary and secondary sources you want to include on your Web site. Which sources best prove your thesis?

Text

The words you write will present your historical analysis and interpretation for your Web site. Although you should include primary sources (possibly text, images, maps, or audio and video files), along with your secondary sources, your words will lead the viewers to a complete understanding of your historical argument.

Good history tells a story, so writing the titles and text for each page and captions for each image and document is an important part of creating your Web site. Like all good writing, your Web site text needs to be grammatically correct, demonstrate good sentence structure, and contain no spelling errors. Be sure to make wise word choices. You should expect to write several drafts. Remember to cite your sources, and add every source to your bibliography.

This simple Web site on the history of a Kansas town maintains clear information.
http://www.rootinaround.com/brainerd/

Don't forget: NHD rules limit you to 1,200 visible, student-composed words. (Citations, code used to build the site, and alternate text tags on images do not count toward the word limit. Primary sources such as oral history interviews, letters, diaries, quotations, and transcriptions of primary documents are not included in the word limit. Captions, source information, and your analysis of the sources do count toward the word limit.) Drafting your text during this step in a word processing program will be much easier than writing it in the Web design program. Select words carefully—move beyond description to focus on historical analysis and interpretation.

Writing for the Web requires you to be brief. Some helpful tips for effective, concise Internet text include the following:

- Create clear, meaningful subheads.
- Use bulleted lists.
- Include one idea per paragraph.
- Use objective, neutral language rather than subjective, boastful, emotional, or exaggerated language.
- Use active voice instead of passive voice.

Many students find it is helpful to arrange their text in layers. You should have a main title for your

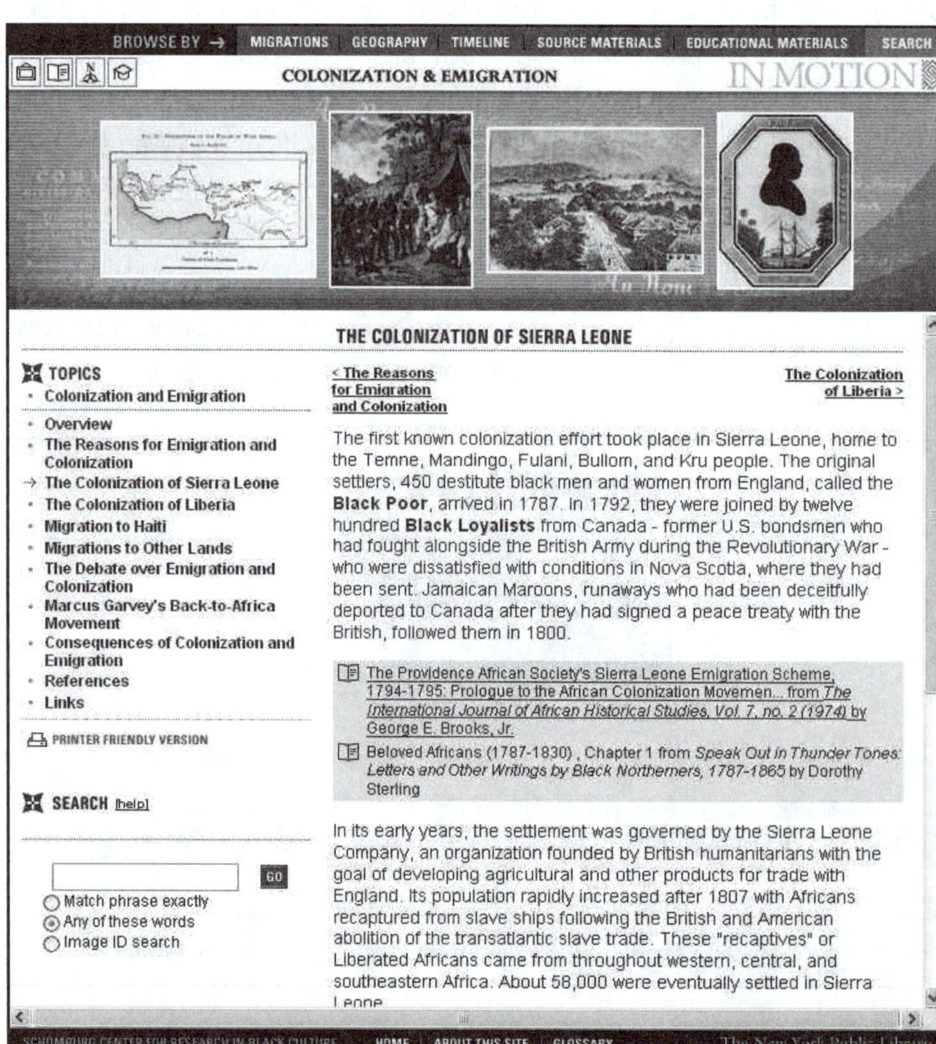

The Schomburg Center for Research in Black Culture's Colonization and Emigration Web site displays several different layers of text: main title, subheads, navigation, body text, and highlighted links to a glossary. Notice the way the primary sources are incorporated into the text. http://www.inmotionaame.org/migrations/topic.cfm?migration=4&topic=3&tab=image

Web site, and it should appear on each page. Then each page should have a header and body text, such as some type of explanatory text or historical analysis. You can also include quotations from primary or secondary sources. Finally, each piece of multimedia or primary source (e.g., image, document, audio/video, map, chart) should include a caption. The type size and placement for a header or caption depends on its importance. Layering your text in this way not only helps someone looking at your Web site to understand it more easily, but it will also help you to choose the two or three main points in your Web site and to think about how they relate to the NHD theme.

Types of Web Text

For more information on the mechanics of text design, see the History Web Site Design section on pages 46–60.

- ***Headline/main title.*** The main headline is the title to your Web site, and it should reflect your topic and argument. Keep it concise but appealing to draw viewers into your Web site. After you find the right title, you'll want to custom design the font, color, and perhaps an image to present the appropriate tone for your Web site. This headline should appear at the top of each page.

- ***Header.*** Each page of your Web site should present a different idea to prove your thesis. Think of it as a subtitle for each page under your main title. Use the same text in your navigation bar so your Web site is consistent. Overly long titles slow down users, so be brief.

You can also use subheads throughout your body text to make reading easier to follow.

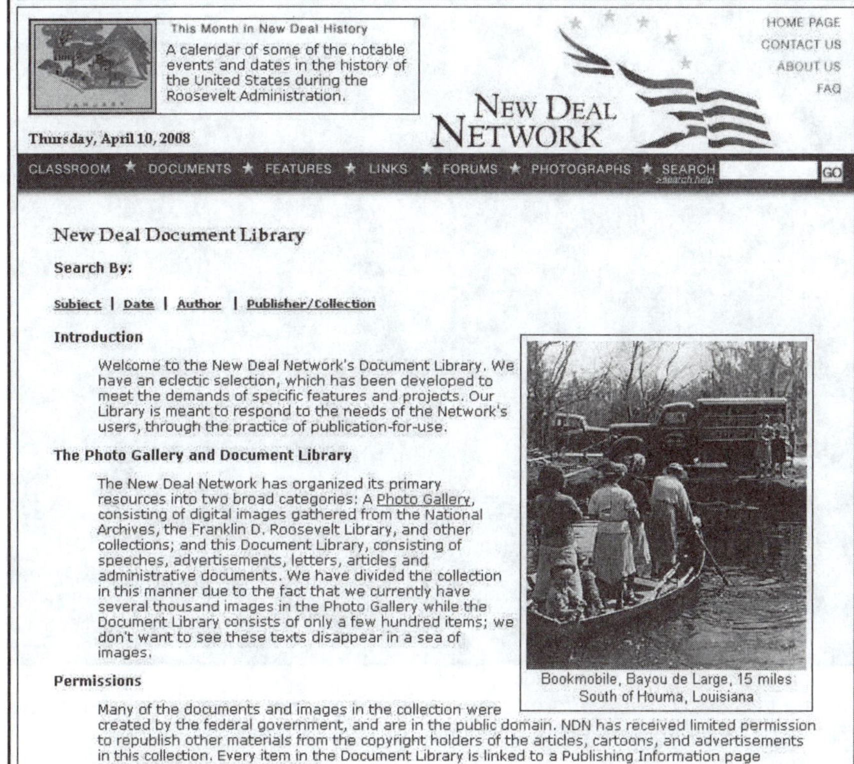

This Month in New Deal History

A calendar of some of the notable events and dates in the history of the United States during the Roosevelt Administration.

HOME PAGE
CONTACT US
ABOUT US
FAQ

NEW DEAL NETWORK

Thursday, April 10, 2008

CLASSROOM ★ DOCUMENTS ★ FEATURES ★ LINKS ★ FORUMS ★ PHOTOGRAPHS ★ SEARCH GO

New Deal Document Library

Search By:

Subject | Date | Author | Publisher/Collection

Introduction

Welcome to the New Deal Network's Document Library. We have an eclectic selection, which has been developed to meet the demands of specific features and projects. Our Library is meant to respond to the needs of the Network's users, through the practice of publication-for-use.

The Photo Gallery and Document Library

The New Deal Network has organized its primary resources into two broad categories: A Photo Gallery, consisting of digital images gathered from the National Archives, the Franklin D. Roosevelt Library, and other collections; and this Document Library, consisting of speeches, advertisements, letters, articles and administrative documents. We have divided the collection in this manner due to the fact that we currently have several thousand images in the Photo Gallery while the Document Library consists of only a few hundred items; we don't want to see these texts disappear in a sea of images.

Bookmobile, Bayou de Large, 15 miles South of Houma, Louisiana

Permissions

Many of the documents and images in the collection were created by the federal government, and are in the public domain. NDN has received limited permission to republish other materials from the copyright holders of the articles, cartoons, and advertisements in this collection. Every item in the Document Library is linked to a Publishing Information page containing copyright information.

New Deal Network has made every effort to trace the ownership of all copyrighted material, and to secure permission from the holders of the copyright. If we have failed to acknowledge any copyright holder, we apologize for the inadvertent error, and will be happy to make the necessary corrections.

The New Deal Network's Document Library makes good use of subheads and explanatory body text. http://newdeal.feri.org/texts/default.cfm

- ***Body text.*** This makes up the bulk of text you write for your Web site and includes your historical descriptions, interpretations, and argument. Be clear and concise. Writing for the Internet is different from writing a paper. It is more difficult to read long passages on screen, so keep your paragraphs short. Remember, make one point per paragraph, and keep the main ideas in the first sentence.

- ***Hook.*** Use a hook to engage your viewers at the top of your text. Also, use the inverted pyramid structure like you would find in a newspaper—the main points are clear and are presented first. Make sure your five Ws and H (who, what, why, when, where, and how)—the description—are near the top. Then narrow down to your analysis and interpretation—the "so what." Newspapers generally fold in half and the top half is visible when newspapers are displayed for sale. The content "above the fold" is the content that is designed especially to attract readers. Similarly, on a Web site, place the most important information "above the fold" or at the top of the first screen. The less a viewer has to scroll down to find the key points, the better.

- ***Voice.*** Use an active voice. Instead of "The document can be downloaded here," for example, write "Download the document here." Make your writing compelling and energetic. Avoid dialect and slang. Be precise with your language. Proofread your text, both for spelling and grammar. Have a teacher, parent, or friend who is unfamiliar with your Web site read your textual content with fresh eyes. Make sure everything is clear and makes sense to your outside reader. You may also want to have a professional expert on your topic read through your text for accuracy.

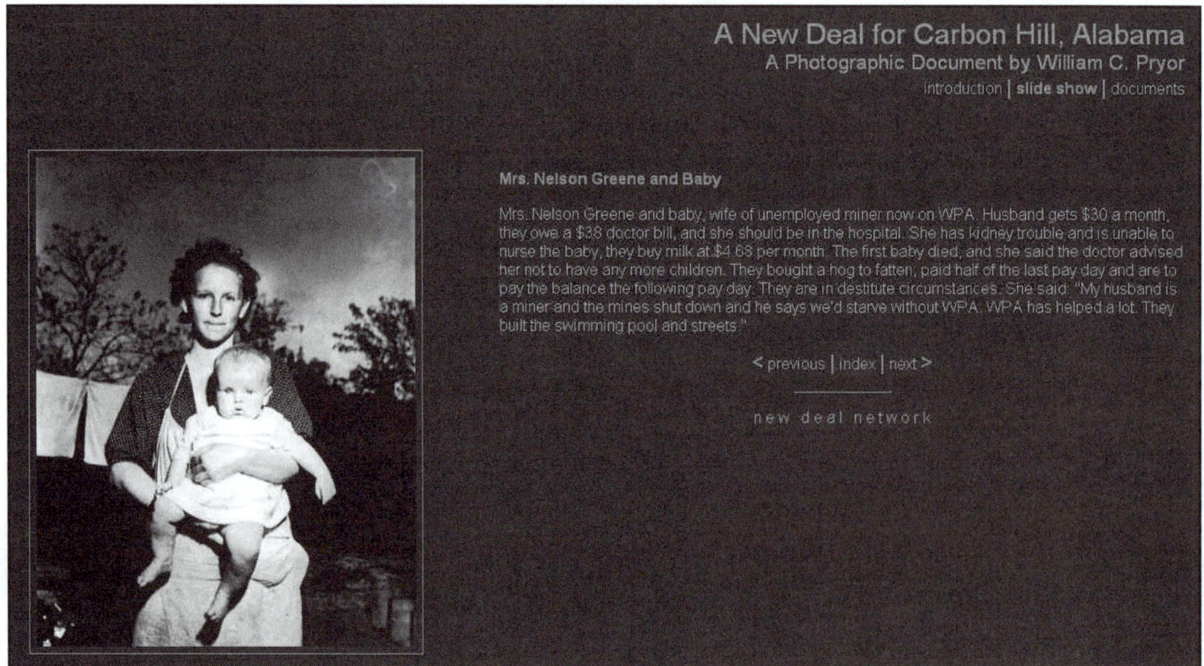

This New Deal photograph documentary includes valuable information in the captions. Note that it is more difficult to read the light reverse print on the dark background than black text on a light background.
http://newdeal.feri.org/carbonhill/k93.htm

- ***Quotations.*** Many contestants display historical quotations from primary sources on their Web sites. Quotes can add excitement, drama, and a sense of the immediacy of past events. Words from quotations do not count against your 1,200-word limit, but avoid using historical quotes as a way to get around the contest word limit. A well-placed quote with accompanying analysis helps guide the viewer through your site and understand your analysis. Using too many quotes and not tying them together will make your Web site look crowded and may not support your argument or thesis.
- ***Captions.*** Each image, map, chart, or primary or secondary document presented on your Web site should include an adjacent caption with brief explanatory source information, such as title and date. As in all NHD categories, you must give credit for and make apparent which materials are not yours, such as quotes, illustrations, media, and movies. These materials should have complete citations in the annotated bibliography. Your captions can also provide sound description, historical analysis, and interpretation without going into too much detail and using too many words by stating the obvious. You may want to discuss what is not shown, what biases are evident, and what information the item provides for your argument. Note also if you have altered the image or document in any way.

Multimedia/Interactive Content

One of the benefits of a Web site is that you can include a variety of formats: documents, artifacts, oral history selections, photographs, paintings, images, maps, time lines, charts, graphs, video clips, audio clips, podcasts, songs, documents, artifacts, newspaper articles, or recorded interviews in addition to the text. You may use such items as professional photographs, graphics, video, recorded music within your site. However, you must give proper credit with the file on the page and in the annotated bibliography.

As you've done your research, you have started to collect these kinds of primary sources to include on your Web site. Now it's time to decide how and where they will fit in on each page. Interactive elements, media, and other non-textual materials that are woven into the text make your Web site unique. Remember: There is no limit to the number of multimedia clips you use, but a single multimedia clip can be no longer than 45 seconds and you have an overall size limit of 100 MB for the entire Web site.

Focus on the features that will distinguish your Web site. What will best illustrate or prove your thesis? What is absolutely necessary, and what would be a nice addition? For a site on westward expansion, for instance, you may want an interactive "zoomable" map that visitors can click to explore different areas involved in the movement west. You may want to embed a video clip, audio clip, or a slideshow to visually or orally illustrate your thesis. To serve a diverse audience, you may want a pop-up glossary of terms or definitions that your viewer can use according to his or her own needs. Make sure your video and audio elements do not distract the viewer or move viewers away from your thesis. Do not include multimedia simply because you found something interesting or flashy. Focus on your history question first and then what technology will best solve these problems. Make sure you can explain why the element will help support your thesis. Have a reason for everything.

Once you have a list of multimedia and interactive features, arrange them in order of priority. Which features do you absolutely need? Which features do you know how to create or could you learn to create?

Recognize how much effort (including technological complexity and time) each feature will require, and decide if it is worth the investment. You may want to keep your Web site simple with solid information and design.

Make sure your multimedia elements help interpret your topic and allow the viewer to participate in interactive ways. Multimedia elements should give the viewer a better understanding of the information and ideas you're presenting. For example, if you are researching the Napoleonic Wars, an interactive map that follows the path of the regiments will help the viewer understand where the events you're describing took place. On the other hand, a quiz that simply reviews factual information found elsewhere in the site would not interpret your topic because it would not provide the audience with new analysis.

You don't have to be a professional Web designer or have years of experience to incorporate interactive, multimedia elements into your Web site. Check out other history Web sites to see how they engage their viewers. Your interactive, multimedia elements could be as simple as a link to a primary source contained in the analysis on your site (e.g., a newspaper article, a letter, an oral history) or a pop-up window with a larger, zoomable version of your source. Remember to include any necessary information or directions for your viewer to access your primary sources.

Images

There are three ways to obtain images for your Web site:

- Copy the image from a Web site on the Internet (note the source of the original image and the Web site where you found the image for your bibliography). Make sure the Web site is a credible source.
- Scan the image from an original document, an image at an archive, or from a book. Be sure to follow the library's policies for scanning. Although a digital image can be created quickly and easily with a good scanner, a digitized manuscript cannot be searched or manipulated the way typed text can be. You may want to include your own transcript in addition to your digitized document. Image files are much larger than text files, and the size and resolution of the

CREATIVE USES OF MULTIMEDIA

- Think about the example of an interactive map that follows Napoleon's path. You could design a map that would allow the viewer to click on battle locations. Maybe a window pops up giving you a historic photo of that location. Maybe the pop-up window includes a letter that a soldier wrote from that battle site. Your job would be to put these things together and then explain their significance. Does the letter discuss the conditions of that location?
- For a Web site about the Black Hawk War, for example, you may want to include portions of the 1804 treaty between the government and two representatives of the Sauk nation. The treaty set the stage for the conflict that occurred 25 years later and is an important part of the Black Hawk War story. Links on key words in the document could take viewers to a more detailed explanation of individual words or ideas.

image can sometimes cause problems with clarity.

- Take a digital picture, then upload your images to your Web site. You may need to manipulate your picture by cropping out what is not necessary.

Before you scan documents or images for use on your Web site, check the settings in the scanning software, especially the settings for resolution and format. You may want to scan the images initially at a high resolution (300 dpi) and in 24-bit color so you can manipulate them if necessary in a photo-editing program, but when you save images to your Web site, you only need to save them at 72 dpi. Save your images as .gif (better for simple graphics, cartoons, or other images with subtle changes in shade or color) or .jpg (JPEGs save images at smaller sizes and still produce nice renderings). NHD asks that you do not use TIFF or Paint files.

Remember that the slimmer or smaller your files are, the easier they will be for your viewers to open. If the resolution is too high, the file will be large and will take a long time to load. However, if the resolution is too low, the image will appear pixilated and fuzzy. Also, remember that not every Web browser will open images in the same way. Test your site on several different computers in different browsers. Think about what you want to show with this image. Do you want to show the full image or do you want to crop the image to highlight a special feature, such as a nugget from the Gold Rush or a servant in the corner of a photograph? Set your image to a size that will not require the viewer to scroll over or down to see all of the image. Do not sacrifice quality, but remember that you have a size limit.

You may want to use graphics to support your historical analysis. Bar graphs, pie charts, census statistics, and other visual representations of information can effectively communicate some ideas and allow your viewers to draw their own conclusions. You can create your own or you can use existing graphics that you may find, as long as you give the creator proper credit. Choose graphics that enhance your argument, concisely display complex information, or provide appropriate, helpful, additional information that cannot be found in your text. Try not to clutter your Web

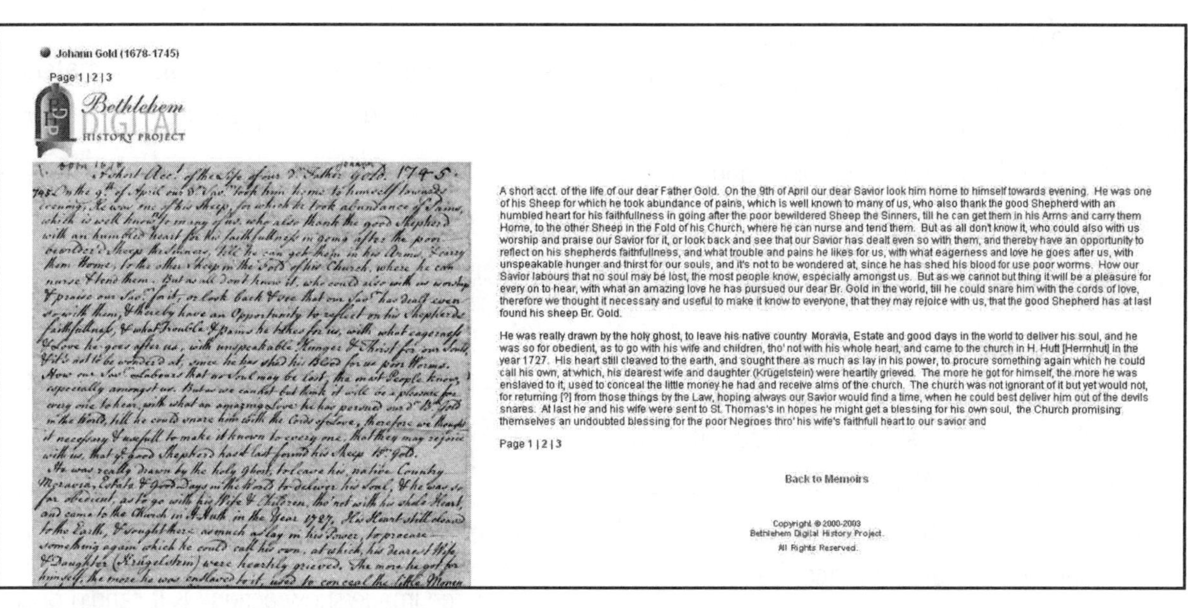

The Bethlehem Digital History Project displays an image of the primary source alongside a transcript that is easier to read and search. http://bdhp.moravian.edu/personal_papers/memoirs/gold/gold1.html

site with too much information. Use captions or titles to explain charts or maps and clearly identify the creator of the graphic. Remember that everything you include should enhance your thesis.

Audio and Video Clips

You can also include audio and moving images on your Web site. These files could be something you create on your own or something created by someone else, again, as long as you provide proper credit. A single multimedia clip may not last more than 45 seconds and may not include student-composed narration. You may conduct your own audio or video interviews with scholars or participants, but the focus should be on their words, not yours. Your title and caption can provide important information about what questions you asked or how you framed the topic.

Check your video editing software for methods of compressing your file to fit the size limit of 100 MB, and be sure to include a link with free, secure, and legal downloads for media players needed to view your clips (such as Flash, QuickTime, or Real Player). If you find a file on the Internet that you want to use on your Web site, you cannot merely provide a link. You must first capture the file or download it to your computer, saving it to the correct folder and page to upload appropriately.

Selecting Items for Display on Your Web Site

You won't be able to use all the materials you find while doing your research. So how do you decide what to include in your Web site and what to leave out? What makes a document, photograph, or object ideal for a Web site? Professional Web developers face the same kinds of choices. Here are some questions to ask as you conduct research and select items to display.

- Does the item fit with the NHD theme and the theme of your Web site?
- Does the item advance the story you are trying to tell? Does it fit with one of your points?
- Is the document you are thinking of displaying easy to read and understand or is it long and wordy? Will it take up too much space on the Web site?
- Is the item visually interesting? Does it contain a famous signature?
- Is the document handwritten or typed? (Handwritten documents provide a connection to a person or event, but typed documents are easier to read.)
- Does the document or photo have color or take an unusual form—for example, a panoramic photograph or a colorful certificate?
- Does a document have unusual markings, such as a seal, letterhead, handwritten comments in the margins, or a "Top Secret" stamp? For example, see page 39.
- What photographs or other visual materials are you considering displaying?
- What kind of information can you get from a photograph, painting, or drawing that is different from a written document?
- What makes you want to look at an image and study it rather than just glance at it quickly and move on to the next item?
- Does a person's face or gestures tell you something about his or her personality or character?
- Does the image show action? Is it candid or is it posed? For example, what might you learn from a photograph of two people shaking hands?

- What is the interaction or the occasion? Who is the audience for this event? If using a photo of a battle, a protest march, or a rescue, think about where the photographer was located and what is being included and excluded from the photograph. Use the caption to point out the relevant features or questions regarding this photograph and the text to explain how this source connects to your larger argument.

Remember to pay strict attention to your topic. Can you find a map or an image that comes directly from your time period? If you are creating a Web site on the colonial Bahamas, for instance, a map made in 1760 (a primary source) would provide more information on the thoughts and world view of 18th-century mapmakers than a map of the colonial Bahamas that was created in 1970 (a secondary source). You won't find photographs on a Web site about the Lewis and Clark expedition simply because photography was not invented until many years later, but plenty of drawings, paintings, and maps exist.

Do you want to include images of artifacts on your Web site, such as a child's toy, a cannonball, or one of the many crafts created in the effort to achieve flight? Will they be historical artifacts or something you build, such as a model?

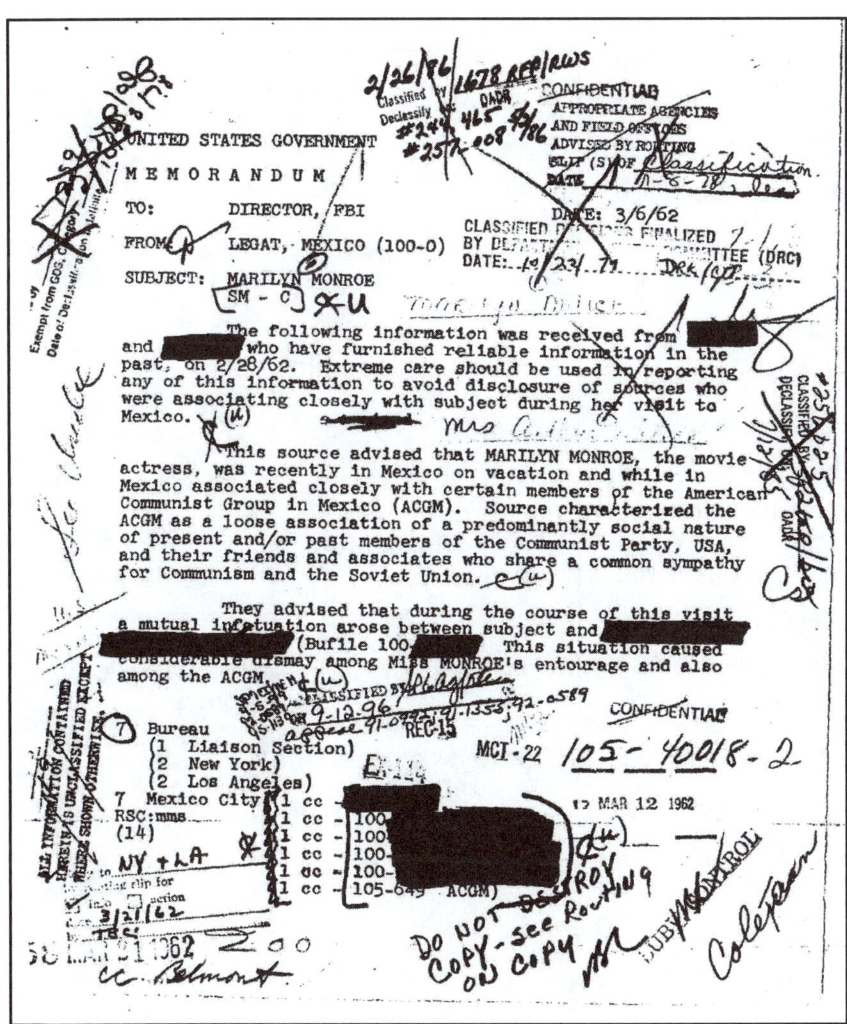

CONFIDENTIAL

APPROPRIATE AGENCIES AND FIELD OFFICES ADVISED BY ROUTING SLIP (S) OF Classification DATE

UNITED STATES GOVERNMENT

MEMORANDUM

TO: DIRECTOR, FBI

FROM: LEGAT, MEXICO (100-0)

SUBJECT: MARILYN MONROE SM - C

DATE: 3/6/62

The following information was received from [redacted] and [redacted] who have furnished reliable information in the past, on 2/28/62. Extreme care should be used in reporting any of this information to avoid disclosure of sources who were associating closely with subject during her visit to Mexico. (u)

This source advised that MARILYN MONROE, the movie actress, was recently in Mexico on vacation and while in Mexico associated closely with certain members of the American Communist Group in Mexico (ACGM). Source characterized the ACGM as a loose association of a predominantly social nature of present and/or past members of the Communist Party, USA, and their friends and associates who share a common sympathy for Communism and the Soviet Union. (u)

They advised that during the course of this visit a mutual infatuation arose between subject and [redacted] (Bufile 100-[redacted]) This situation caused considerable dismay among Miss MONROE's entourage and also among the ACGM. (u)

CONFIDENTIAL

7 Bureau
(1 Liaison Section)
(2 New York)
(2 Los Angeles)
7 Mexico City (1 cc - [redacted]
1 cc - 100[redacted]
1 cc - 100[redacted]
1 cc - 100[redacted]
1 cc - 100-[redacted]
1 cc - 105-649 ACGM)
RSC:mms
(14)

MCI-22 105-40018-2

REC-15

MAR 12 1962

DO NOT DESTROY COPY - SEE ROUTING ON COPY

cc Belmont

The Federal Bureau of Investigation's (FBI) online archive includes documents that have been heavily edited, such as this memo regarding Marilyn Monroe. The editing makes for interesting visual information.
http://foia.fbi.gov/foiaindex/monroe.htm

HISTORY WEB SITE ORGANIZATION

Now that you have selected your Web site topic, done some research, and narrowed in on the content of your Web site, it is time to design the organization of your Web site. Remember, your Web site must contain a home page and other pages, all linked. Part of the benefit of a Web site over another NHD category is that it is interactive, which means it can present materials in many formats and the viewer can choose his or her path through the material. Your organization can be linear or topical. The important thing is that every page on your Web site needs to connect to your argument in a new way. It may help to fine-tune your topic and decide the main points you want to present on each page.

There are many decisions to make about how to divide your research and argument into different pages on your site. Time, location, topic, and size are just a few of the general categories into which you can sort information. The way you organize the information can help you make different arguments. For example, a Web site about the Civil War could be organized chronologically, by battle, or by groups of people involved in the conflict. How would each of these organizations help or hinder a viewer's understanding of the topic?

To begin, think about your information as if you were writing an outline for a paper. How would you divide up your material into major sections? How does each section support your argument? Now think of another way you could divide the information (e.g., chronologically, topically, geographically). Which system will make more sense to your viewer? No matter how you choose to divide your information into separate Web pages, each page should fit together to support your thesis. How do the ideas on each page connect to the others?

Remember: You're not just building different Web pages, you're building a Web site. You have to give your site an overall organization that is logical and easy to navigate. There are many ways to do this, and building your site on paper first will give you a chance to play with these organizational structures before you put time and energy into construction. Here are a few examples:

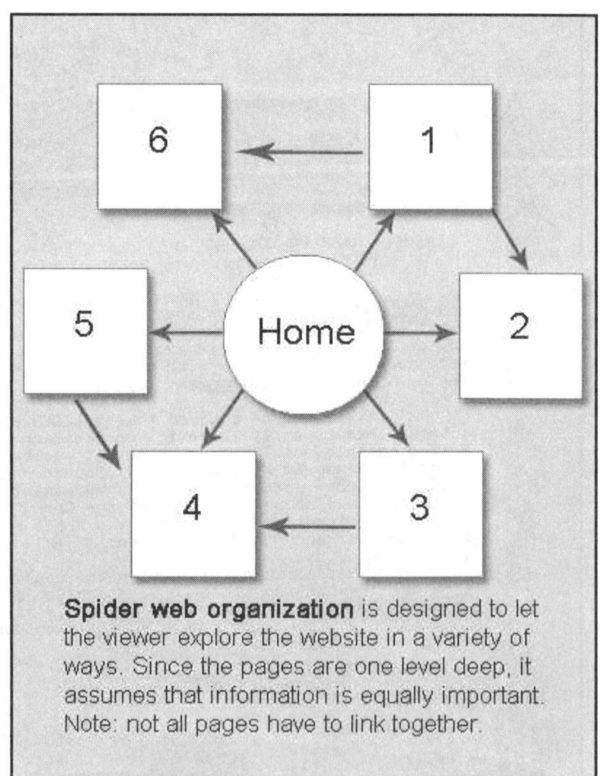

Spider web organization is designed to let the viewer explore the website in a variety of ways. Since the pages are one level deep, it assumes that information is equally important. Note: not all pages have to link together.

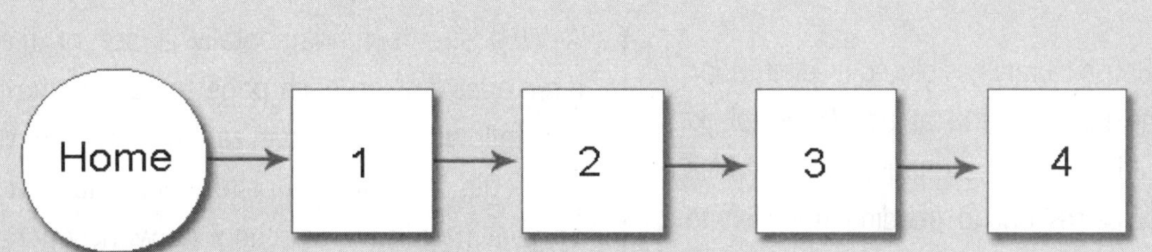

Linear organization assumes that a viewer is going to go from one page to the next in a very specific order. For example, if your website were examining a four-day battle in the Civil War, and you had one page for each day, you would assume that your viewer would start with the first day and move forward. You would still link all four days in the navigation bar on each page, allowing the viewer to jump ahead or backward.

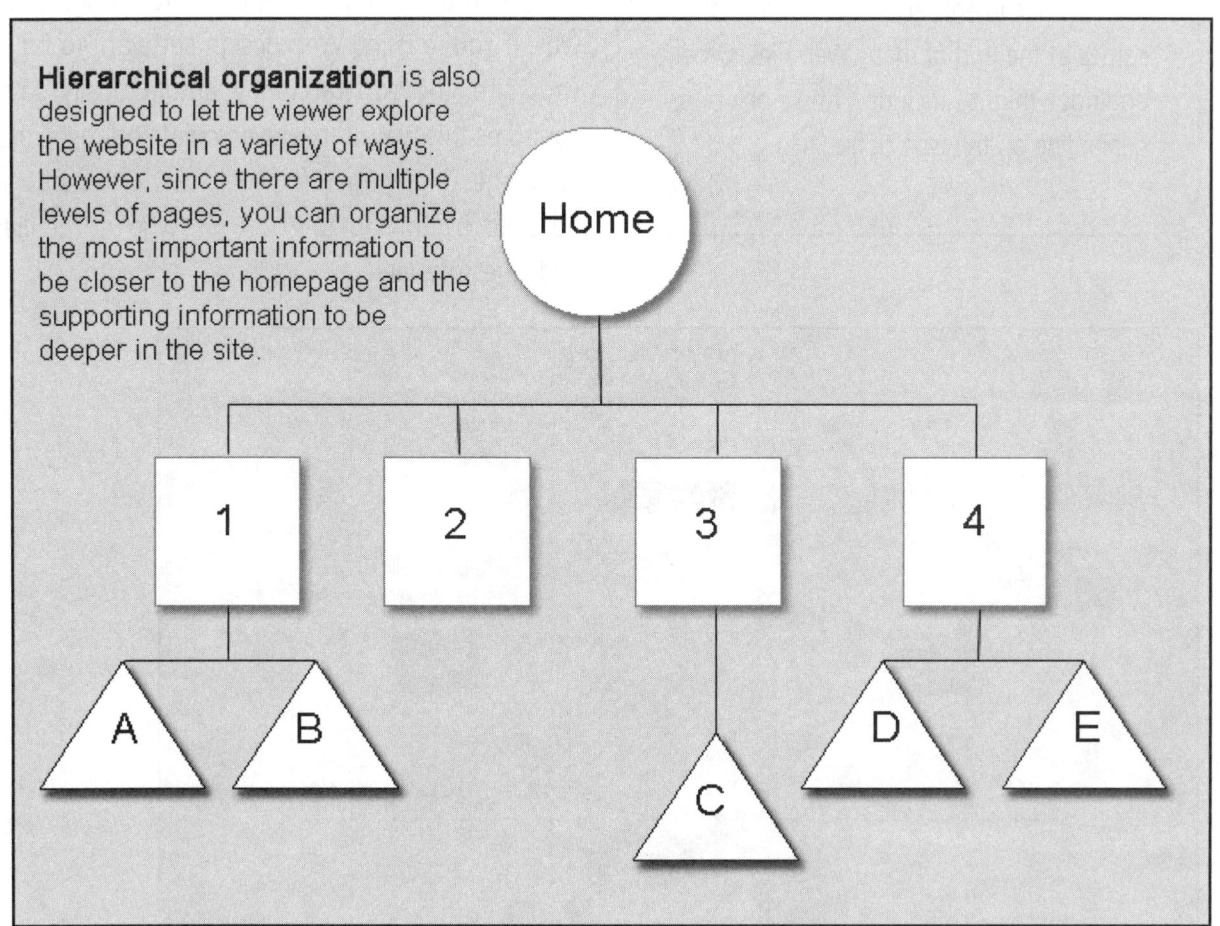

Hierarchical organization is also designed to let the viewer explore the website in a variety of ways. However, since there are multiple levels of pages, you can organize the most important information to be closer to the homepage and the supporting information to be deeper in the site.

FILE ADDRESSES

The British Library has placed its digitization of the Magna Carta at http://www.bl.uk/collections/treasures/magna.html, which nicely parses out to (reading from left to right) the Web server of the British Library (in the United Kingdom, of course), in their collections division directory, in the special "treasures" directory of the collections division (where the Magna Carta surely belongs), followed by the first word of the famous document and the ".html" that comes at the end of many Web files. Other endings might include htm or php, depending on the type of file.

Files

A Web site is fundamentally a set of files or directories, linking each page to your home page and following your organizational scheme. When you begin designing your site, start a master folder on your hard drive or school network where you will store all the HTML files, images, and media that you plan to use in your site and nothing else.

Good sites sort themselves out and make their logical structure apparent through well-named directories and files. Keep your Web site organized and clean by saving files in a natural, progressive way. If you're using Web design software to build your site, the software may automatically save your files this way. It may even create relative links to images and pages for you. Check this out in advance by talking to someone who is familiar with the software.

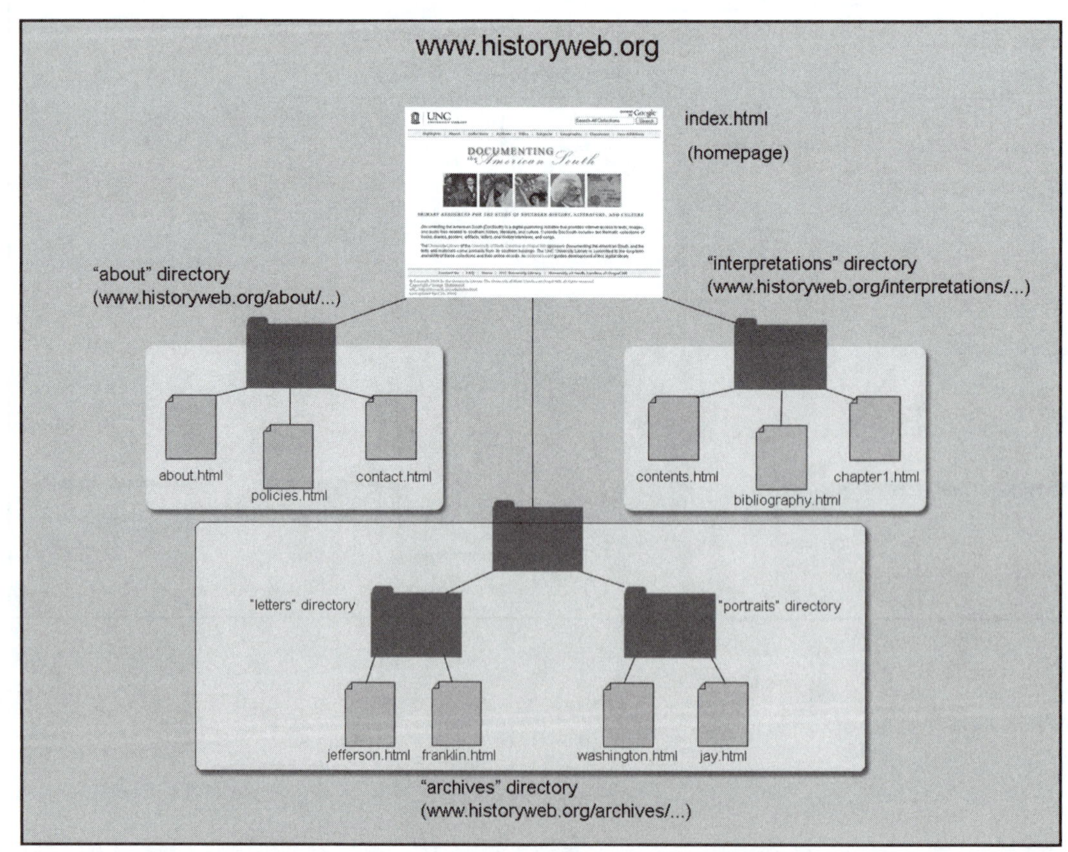

Example of a site map or file structure for a Web site.

At the "top" of this hierarchy of directories and files, and providing an entrance to all of the others, is the home page, which should be saved with the name "index.html." A diagram of a Web site's basic structure can look like a genealogical tree, where a parent is a directory with children that are individual Web pages.

Each page should have its own folder, including images and any other files. Put all of your images in an image folder associated with each page. Name each folder (and each page) something clear and simple. So that they will function properly on all types of computers, use lowercase letters for your directory and file names, and leave out spaces or any symbols other than underscores and dashes. The path of your files will then become the Web address for your pages. Each URL slash (/) indicates that the directory or file to the right of the slash resides inside of the directory named to the left of the slash.

All pages must be interconnected with hyperlinks. Using relative links instead of absolute links will help if you move items from system to system. Double and triple check to make sure all your links work properly.

To refer to an image in an images folder, you will need to provide the proper path name (your Web design software may do this automatically). For example, here is the path name of an image link: <img src="C:\school\nhd\cows\cheese.jpg">. This particular path name tells the browser to go to the hard drive of that computer (C:) to find the folder "school," then to the folder "nhd," and then to the folder "cows" for an image called cheese.jpg.

As you build your site, link only to files in that folder and use relative path names in your links. This will make it much easier to submit your project for competitions because you can upload the entire folder without having to move individual files that might break your links. Your Web site must be saved in a root directory of your file with the name "index" so that it is easy for your viewer to find.

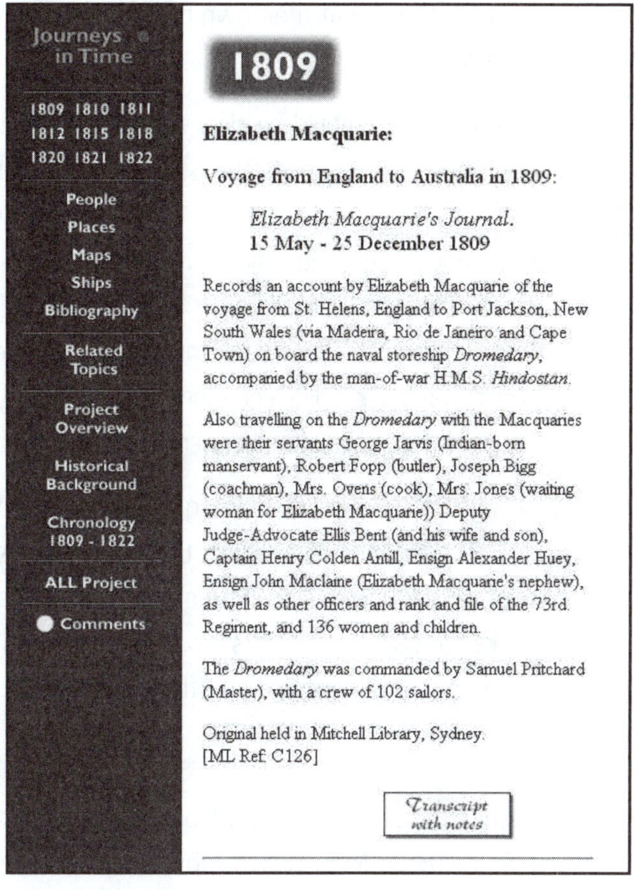

The Macquarie University Library's "Journey in Time" project demonstrates clear, simple navigation. http://www.lib.mq.edu.au/all/journeys/1809/

Navigation

Plan your Web site's navigation carefully to make it accessible to your viewers. You should include some basic navigation tools on each page of your Web site. Common to most Web sites is some way to get back to the home page (for instance, by clicking on the main headline or title at the top); links to other main sections of the site; or links to pages with credits. No matter how you organize the pages of your Web site, you can make it easily accessible by providing a menu on every page. Viewers should be able to move through the site at their own pace and along their own path.

Your hyperlinks should be clear and easy to find. You don't need to include phrases such as "Click here to return to the home page" or "Click here to see a transcript of the document." Simply design your navigation tools so your viewer will know to click on "Home page" or "Transcript." You may want to design your hyperlinks as a different color than regular body text and to change color after the user has viewed the page.

Navigation should be an integral part of your Web site design and it can help unify the Web site's overall look across a multitude of individual pages. Make sure all of your links work. Test every link on different computers and in different browsers.

Size

Remember to follow NHD Web site rules about size and content. NHD has established specific rules about the size of your Web site (100 MB), the use of media devices, and which words count toward your 1,200-word limit. If you violate these rules, judges will penalize your entry. However, within these rules you have a lot of room to be creative. For more about the rules in the Web site category, go to http://www.nhd.org/images/uploads/library/WebRules_v4.pdf.

Web Site Storyboard

A storyboard is a visual plan for your Web site. It usually consists of a series of pages that include a rough sketch outlining the content, navigation, and design elements of your Web site. Taking time to storyboard early in the process will save time in the long run and make a more solid site. Before you start designing your pages and using design software programs, create a storyboard to collect your information and organize your topics.

Lay out each topic with a different storyboard. This will break down your Web site into manageable pieces, both for you and for your viewer. Think about how the viewers will navigate between topics.

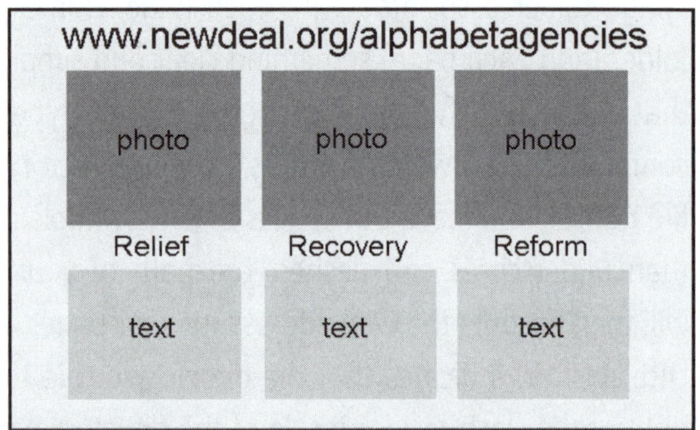

A sketch of a page's design will help you determine what kinds of images, text, and font to plan.

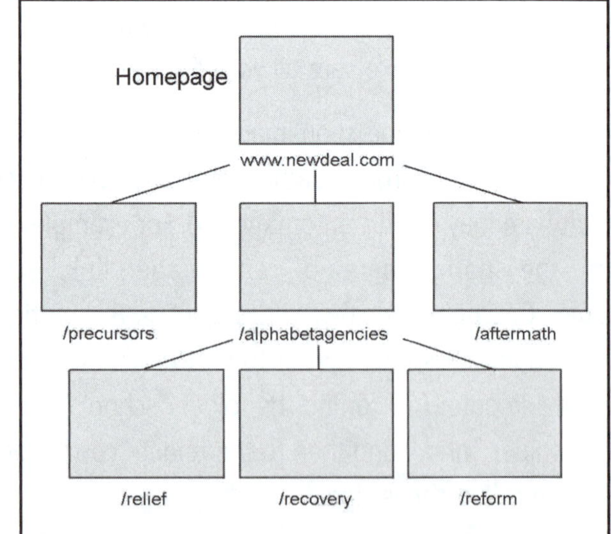

A simple storyboard demonstrates how each page of a Web site fits with the other pages into the site's purpose.

WEB SITE CONTENT STORYBOARD

- What is your topic?
- What is your thesis? What is your angle or argument?
- List the points you want to display on the different pages of your Web site. How does each page provide important analysis for your topic?
- How will you divide your information into Web pages?
- How will you organize these pages within your site? Will you use a linear, spider web, or hierarchical organization (see pages 40–41)?
- Provide the following information for each page:
  - Descriptive title
  - Main heading
  - Subheadings
  - Purpose of the page
  - Description of content
  - Types of images and multimedia
  - Links to other pages
- What text—your own historical analysis—will be included on each page? Type out your text.
- List all primary sources (e.g., images, documents, maps, newspapers) you will include on each page.
- What secondary sources will you include on each page? This may include maps, charts, quotes from historians, or time lines that you create, which will become secondary material.
- Create a Web site storyboard. Sketch (either on paper or electronically) what you want to put on each page and how the pages will be linked.

HISTORY WEB SITE DESIGN

Web sites communicate through more than just the items you select and the words you write. Color, form, legibility, size, line, font, texture, and space are all tools you can use to improve your Web site's presentation and to communicate your topic and argument. This doesn't mean your site design and construction have to be expensive or fancy. Often a clean, simple design works best. You will be judged on how your design supports the clarity of your presentation—that is, how you organize your material; the visual impact of your site; your effectiveness in displaying your argument with documents, photographs, maps, and other illustrations; and your analysis. Your Web design needs to support your topic but not overwhelm its content.

Content is more important than glitz. Computers can do a lot of cool things, but think about the NHD criteria and remember the most important elements of your Web site: analysis, historical context, and connection to theme. To make these ideas clear for your viewer, focus on a Web site design that is easy to read and understand. Do not use decorative animation and keep clip art to an absolute minimum. Avoid busy background images and other clutter. It's also a good idea to include some blank space in your pages so the viewer isn't overwhelmed.

You may want to sketch out on paper several design ideas and get feedback from family, friends, and teachers. Keep a storyboard of your Web site, both for content and for design. Show placement of text, images, multimedia, graphics, and hyperlinks. It's easier to move things around on paper than on a computer. Create a calendar of deadlines for each design component of your Web site.

Design Help: Software and Templates

Software designed specifically to produce a Web site runs on your personal computer and allows you to build pages before uploading them to a server. There are a number of programs for creating basic Web sites with texts and images; they range in price from free to expensive. Also helpful are software programs that allow you to generate, alter, and enhance photographs, line drawings, decorative text, and complex graphics. You can resize, crop, and compress images for your Web site.

Many computer programs can help you create the files that make up basic Web sites. These programs require varying levels of HTML or other technical knowledge. Many programs that were not designed for Web production now allow users to save files as Web pages, without knowledge of HTML or a cascading style sheet (CSS). For instance, Microsoft Word, Excel, and PowerPoint have added a "save as web page" feature. Although they may be less sophisticated than Web pages designed from scratch, such pages are viewable on the Internet with little fuss.

Many Web design software programs include templates to build Web sites. You are more than welcome to use a template for your NHD Web site. You may want to make a few minor changes to the design to fit your topic and time period, or you may want to design your own site using CSS according to your own abilities. When borrowing or using someone else's coding or scripting, however, you should give credit just as you would with other materials. Please note that the credit for these materials must be given in a manner that is visible to the average user, not just in the code itself. You are not required to use elaborate, expensive software programs. Several free products are available to download, or you can also build your Web site in notepad using HTML code.

HTML Basics

HTML is the language of Web creation. It's a simple, universal markup language that allows Web site builders to create complex pages of text and images that can be viewed by anyone else on the Internet, regardless of what kind of computer or browser is being used. HTML is basically a series of tags that are integrated into a text document. They're a lot like architectural plans—silently telling the browser what to do and how to display the finished product. If you use Web design software, you may not even need to use HTML coding, although it's good to understand how it works.

The file sent by a Web server generally consists of regular text surrounded by HTML passages that tell a browser how to format the regular text, point to other Web pages (through links), and request additional materials (e.g., images) from the server to complete the page. The simple but elegant idea behind HTML is thus to "wrap" passages of text with text markers, or tags, that identify the passage's contents, much like the front and back cover help to identify the contents of a book. The angle brackets < > signal the tag format, and the backslash symbol / indicates the end of that format. For example, <p> begins a new paragraph, and </p> ends the paragraph. Tags must travel in pairs to mark the beginning and ending of the enclosed information in the right way.

A basic HTML page begins with the tag <html> and ends with </html>. In between, the file has two sections, the header and the body. The header, enclosed with <header> and </header>, contains information about the page that won't actually appear on the page itself, such as the title. The body—<body> and </body>—is where the page content is. Everything that appears on the page is contained with these tags.

HTML Cheatsheet

<html></html> Creates an HTML document

<head></head> Sets off the title and other information that isn't displayed on the Web page itself

<body></body> Sets off the visible portion of the document

<title></title> Puts the name of the document in the title bar

<h1></h1> Creates the largest headline

<h6></h6> Creates the smallest headline

<li></li> List elements

<ol></ol> Ordered list

<ul></ul> Unordered list

<strong></strong> Creates bold text

<em></em> Creates italic text

<a href="URL">text to be linked**</a>** Creates a hyperlink

<p></p> Creates and ends a paragraph

<p align=?/> Aligns a paragraph to the left, right, or center

**
** Inserts a line break

<blockquote></blockquote> Indents text from both sides

<img src="name"/> Adds an image

<hr/> Inserts a horizontal rule

SAMPLE HTML DOCUMENT

```
<!DOCTYPE html PUBLIC "-//W3C//DTD HTML 4.01 Transitional//EN"
 "http://www.w3.org/TR/html4/loose.dtd">
<html>
<head>
 <title>My first HTML document</title>
</head>
<body>
<!— Site navigation menu —>
<ul class="navbar">
 <li><a href="index.html">Home page</a>
 <li><a href="musings.html">Musings</a>
 <li><a href="town.html">My town</a>
 <li><a href="links.html">Links</a>
</ul>
<h1>An important heading</h1>
<p>This is the first paragraph. This is a really <em>interesting</em> topic!
</p>
<img src="peter.jpg" width="200" height="150" alt="My friend Peter">
<h2>A slightly less important heading</h2>
<p>This is the second paragraph. This a link to <a href="peter.html">Peter's page</a>.</p>
</body>
</html>
```

For more information about HTML, see http://www.webmonkey.com/tutorial/Make_an_HTML_Document

CSS

A cascading style sheet (CSS) allows you to manipulate the design of your Web site in one place. CSS is for style, where HTML is for content. This makes it easier to change the color, font, or presentation of each page at once, separate from the actual HTML content of your site. Most Web design software automatically creates a style sheet for you, and you won't have to worry about it unless you want to manipulate it. Like HTML, CSS uses its own language and syntax to divide different categories and classes of Web design elements. With CSS you can control style elements such as margins, padding, text, fonts, anchors/links, backgrounds, borders, lists, width and height, and position. You can measure fonts, borders, padding, and so on in pixels, ems, and percentages. You can order the elements of your Web site into the following groups: body, classes, divisions (divs), and spans. Be sure to link your CSS stylesheet to your HTML document.

For more information, see http://www.webmonkey.com/authoring/stylesheets/tutorials/tutorial.html. For examples of CSS templates, see http://csszengarden.com/. Several other Web sites provide information about CSS with templates, learning modules, tips, and codes. Do a Google search to find pointers online.

CSS Cheatsheet

Each component can be styled in the following ways:

Margins: length, percentage, auto

Padding: length, percentage

Text: color; letter-spacing; text-align; text-decoration; text-indent; text-transform; white-space; word-spacing

Font: font-family; font-size; font-style; font-variant; font-weight

Links: color; visited color; a:hover color

Background: attachment; color; image; position; repeat

Border: color; style; width; border-bottom; border-left; border-right; border-top

Layout

The layout of your Web site should center on your content. Each page should have the same header, linking back to your home page; a navigation bar, either as a sidebar or

SAMPLE CSS DOCUMENT

```
body {
 padding-left: 11em;
 font-family: Georgia, "Times New Roman",
   Times, serif;
 color: purple;
 background-color: #d8da3d }
ul.navbar {
 list-style-type: none;
 padding: 0;
 margin: 0;
 position: absolute;
 top: 2em;
 left: 1em;
 width: 9em }
h1 {
 font-family: Helvetica, Geneva, Arial,
   SunSans-Regular, sans-serif }
ul.navbar li {
 background: white;
 margin: 0.5em 0;
 padding: 0.3em;
 border-right: 1em solid black }
ul.navbar a {
 text-decoration: none }
a:link {
 color: blue }
a:visited {
 color: purple }
address {
 margin-top: 1em;
 padding-top: 1em;
 border-top: thin dotted }
```

The University of Missouri at Kansas City's "They Came to Fight" Web site maintains a simple, clean layout, focusing on powerful images and informative text. http://theycametofight.org/index.html

under your header; main body text with multimedia content, such as images, primary documents, maps, charts, and audiovisual files; and a footer. Keep your layout simple and consistent for each page.

There are several different ways to design the layout of your Web site. Some programs use tables and columns, while others use divisions, or divs. It doesn't matter which method you use for your Web site as long as you are consistent for each page. If you divide your design into columns or tables, make sure each fits the text or images inside each cell.

The key to a good layout is balance. Look at the different elements on your Web site as if they have weight and gravity. The larger items possess more weight than the smaller ones. Imagine a seesaw underneath your page. Does everything balance out evenly across the page? Are your elements evenly distributed? Try not to tip your seesaw with heavier elements on only one side of the page. Do not clutter your layout with unnecessary design, but instead remember to use empty space to balance your Web page. Keep your layout consistent across your Web site. Alignment, proximity, repetition, and contrast all work together to produce a good, clean layout.

Remember the importance of contrast on a Web site—between color, text, images, and blank space. Also, pay attention to proximity. Leave between 3 and 10 pixels of padding space between graphical elements and the block of text for a nice, clean margin. Make sure your captions are close enough to the images to allow viewers to make connections. Check the alignment of your page. Is it easy to follow? Will your viewers be able to move easily from text to image and from page to page? A good Web designer will use related colors, fonts, sizes, and textures to connect various pages on a Web site.

This layout design uses three columns in the same way as effective sites such as the New York Times *Web site.*

Navigation should be an integral part of your site design and can help to unify the site's overall look across multiple pages. Consistent fonts, colors, and icons located in the same position on each page will help the user focus on the content of your Web site.

Typography

There are two main classes of text you need to design. The first is your history description and analysis, or your body text. The second includes headers and titles, which are designed primarily to communicate your topic and time period. Be sure to format your typeface appropriately.

To make your body text more readable, each column of text should be between 300 and 600 pixels wide, for a total of 8 to 16 words per line if you use an average font. Narrower columns will look more like a newspaper, and wider columns will look more like a book. Make your font size reasonable for easy reading. As you prepare text filled with important historical information and analysis for your Web site, remember that it can be difficult to read long passages online. Break up your text into readable chunks. Keep your paragraphs on the shorter side. And remember that

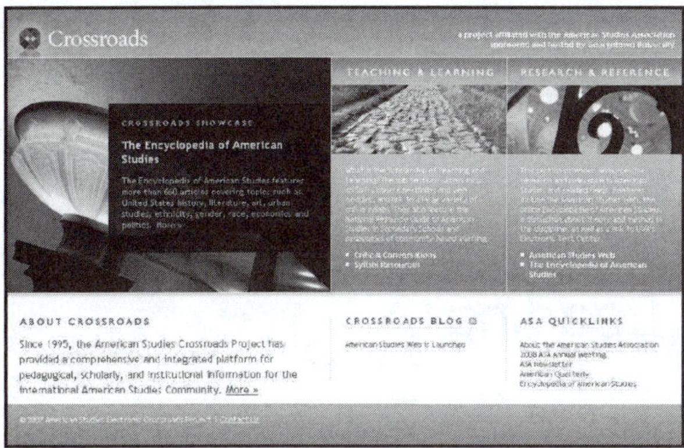

Georgetown University's "Crossroads" Web site maintains three well-balanced columns. http://crossroads.georgetown.edu/

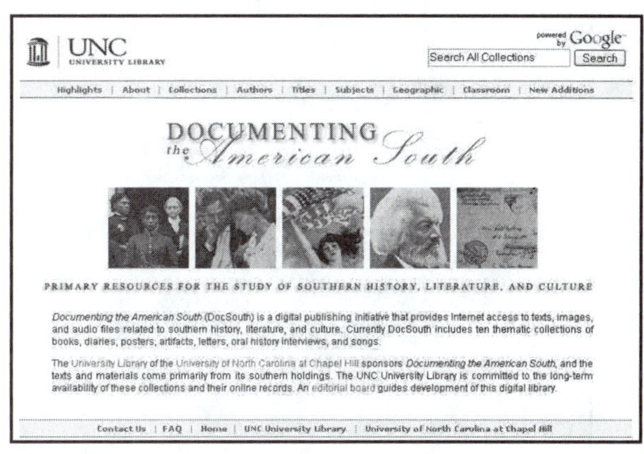

The University of North Carolina's "Documenting the American South" Web site balances a graphic title and well-proportioned images with a wide text box. http://docsouth.unc.edu/

American readers are accustomed to reading text that is aligned to the left margin rather than to the right margin or centered. Do not center your body text.

Be sure to maintain adequate white (or neutral-colored) space around your text to make it easy to read. Reverse text, or type that is white or another color on a black background, is often dramatic and may work well for a header or title, but it is difficult to read for your main Web text. Although the flexibility of the Web permits the text to be any color, only in rare circumstances should you make your text a color other than black (the default color on the Web) or near-black. High contrast makes text easier to read—a main goal in creating your Web site. Check leading and kerning to make your text readable.

Find a font that will display your text clearly. Studies show that sans serif fonts (those without little flourishes at the ends of the letters) are more readable online than serif fonts. Long passages of text look a little crisper on most screens in sans serif and are easier to read in different sizes. You can be more creative with your headline font, which should be saved as an image. Whichever style of font you choose, remember that not all computers share all fonts, so you should choose a common font readable by most computers. Sans serif fonts found on most computers include Verdana, Arial, and Helvetica;

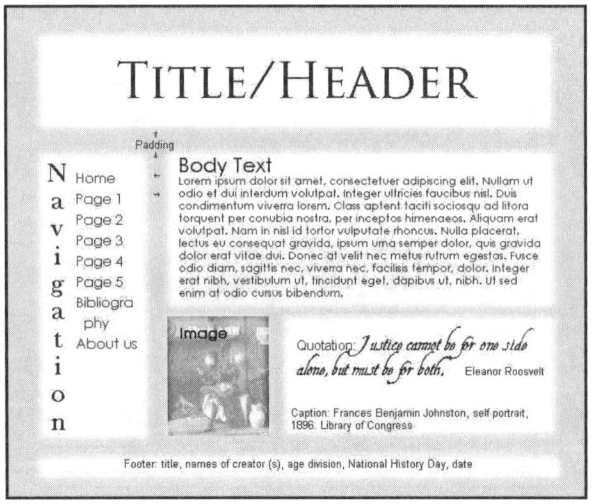

This simple layout demonstrates places for navigation, body text, images, and quotations. Notice the use of fonts.

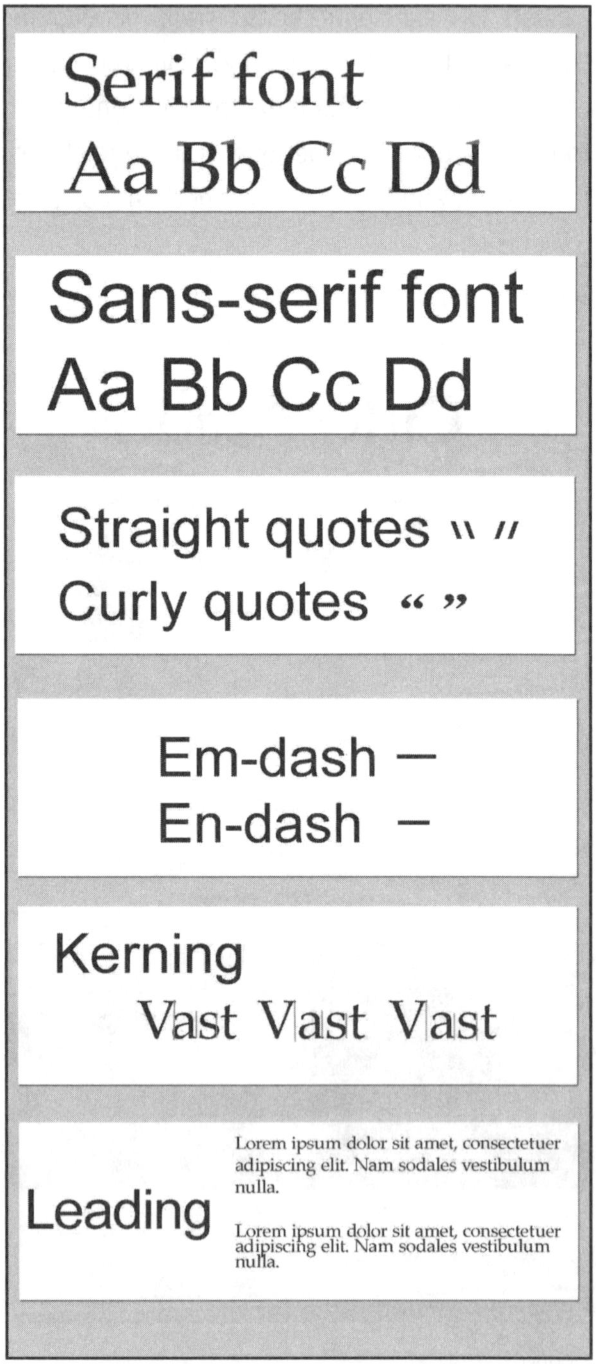

common serif fonts include Times, Times New Roman, and Bookman. Try to avoid monospaced fonts like Courier for main blocks of text (though Courier is nice for suggesting typewritten text if you seek that effect to highlight content).

Use curly quotes instead of straight quotes and em dashes instead of double hyphens.

The Web site title should be larger than your main text and should be placed in a prominent place to draw attention to the topic and the connection with the NHD theme. Choose a typeface that illustrates the time period or topic of your Web site, and save the title as an image so the font will appear on every browser exactly as you designed it. You may want to decorate the title with an image or another graphic that illustrates your Web site's theme. You may choose to follow this main title on your home page with a brief written introduction to the entire Web site.

Section headers. These are slightly smaller than the main Web site title header. They draw attention to important subjects and distinct pages developed on the Web site. Each topic might be followed by student-written text that gives information about the topic and its significance. This body text should be in an easy-to-read font, smaller than the headers but larger than the captions.

Quotations. Pull quotes set aside from regular text will probably have larger font size than the body text but will still be smaller than headers. Their font should be set off from body text and headers as well. You can do this through color, background, font, or graphics, such as lines above and below the quote. If you choose to use a nontraditional font not found on most computers, save your quotation as an image in the font of your choice. Remember, quotations do not count toward your 1,200-word limit.

The Ruined City

It was the completeness of the wreck; the total desolation which met the eye on every hand; the utter blankness of what had a few hours before been so full of life, of associations, of aspirations, of all things which kept the mind of a Chicagoan so contantly driven.

❖Elias Colbert and Everett Chamberlin
Chicago and the Great Conflagration, 1871

- The Burnt District
- Among the Ruins
- Before and After

- The Losses by the Fire
- Chicago by Moonlight

Devastated Chicago remained so hot that it took a day or two before it was possible even to begin a survey of the physical damage. According to the papers, in some instances when anxious businessmen opened their safes among the rubble of what was once their offices, precious contents that had survived the inferno suddenly burst into flame on exposure to the air. Shortly after the fire, Stephen L. Robinson, a North Division resident whose home was not burned, set out with a printed map of the city to mark what was still standing. Among the few scattered survivors he noted were the mansion of Mahlon Ogden (brother of William) on Lafayette (now Walton) Street north of Washington Square Park, and the much more modest home north of Armitage of police officer Richard Bellinger, both of which were saved by a combination of vigilant dousings and good luck. And had he reached the South Division, he would have seen the Lind Block standing a forlorn watch over the downtown. Had he then crossed to the West Division, he would have found the O'Leary cottage safe and sound in front of the ashes of the barn.

The Chicago Historical Society's site on the Great Chicago Fire of 1871 demonstrates good use of quotations, body text, and navigation to other pages using icons. http://www.chicagohs.org/fire/ruin/ index.html

Captions. These should be the smallest size typeface of all the different sizes on your page, although still large enough to read. Captions should accompany every primary source, image, map, or chart. They identify the document or image and go into more detail about the specific item. You should give credit to the institution where the original document can be found. Make sure your captions are clear and easy to read, and keep your font simple.

Citations. Citations—footnotes or endnotes—can include links to your bibliography or to the actual source, if you include it on your Web site. Traditionally, footnotes appear at the bottom of a page. However, with the benefits of the Internet, your users can easily pull up your footnotes into a pop-up window or a separate page with a simple click. There are several ways to present your footnotes:

- Gathered with all notes at the end of the text—endnotes
- Gathered with all notes and linked to a separate page of notes
- Appearing alone in a small pop-up window
- Arranged to one side of the text
- In parentheses immediately after the reference

The citation mark itself, within your body text, serves as a signpost to further information, and can be written into your code as a superscript, in brackets, in a different color, or with specific hover capabilities. Whether your footnote marker itself is a link or just a signal, make sure that it is clear, that it does not distract from your text, and that the user can easily find the footnote information located elsewhere. If you hyperlink the citation mark to the footnote or endnote, be sure to also link the footnote back to the mark to bring your viewer back to the text at the appropriate place. For more information on different note techniques, see http://www.archiva.net/footnote/#.

Color

As a Web designer, you set the mood and tone of your Web site. Color can entice, frighten, persuade, sell, calm, and even inspire. Choose your colors wisely. If you decide to use large areas of color on your Web site, either to differentiate various subsections of a page or as a background, choose an unobtrusive color such as beige, grey, a pastel, or another color against which your text will be easy to

The Chicago Historical Society uses a variety of fonts for the subhead, navigation, and caption. http://www.chicagohs.org/ fire/ruin/library.html

The University of Missouri at Kansas City's "They Came to Fight" Web site allows viewers to click on images and find a pop-up window for this image of Frederick Douglass, with an expanded image, detailed caption, quotation, and source. http://theycametofight.org/historyofresistance.html

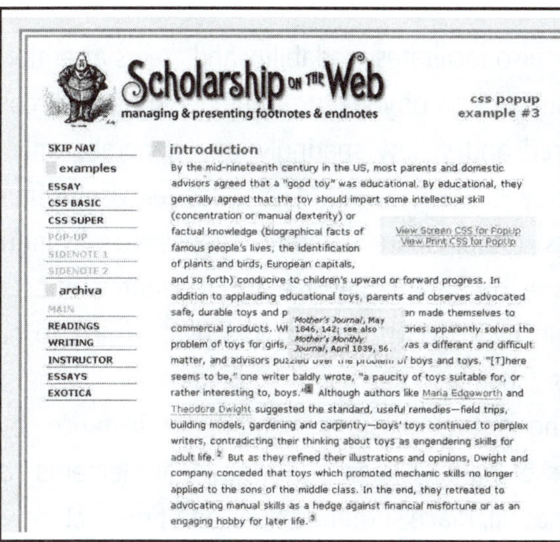

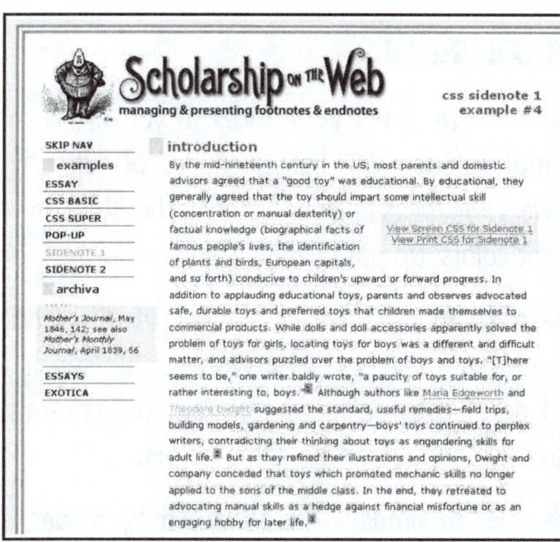

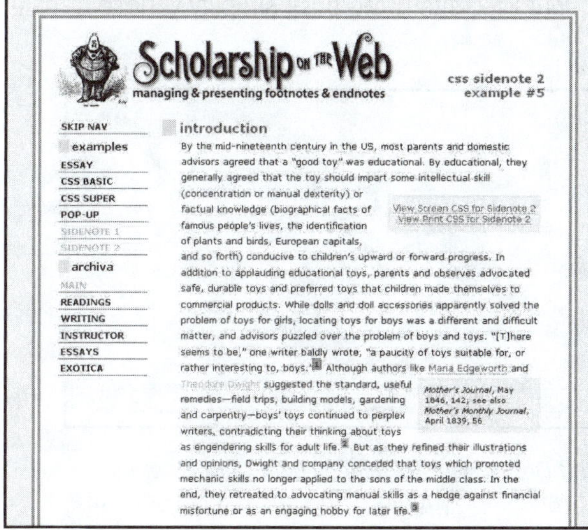

read. The right color can help keep the overall site simple. With a restrained baseline color, images and text will stand out, and the viewer's eyes will be attracted to what's important rather than to the background or page margins. Although HTML makes it possible to have an image as a background (either singular, taking up the whole background, or "tiled," where it repeats across the page), avoid doing so. Background images distract readers and make any overlaid texts harder to read. Because this book is not printed in color, Web site URLs are given to enable you to view the sites online to see the colors used.

Colors can communicate a lot; they can indicate attitude and personality for instance. Choose two or three colors to use on your Web site, with different degrees of shade and tone. The colors you choose for your Web site will connect a mood with your topic.

It is also important to remember texture, juxtaposition, and amount of color. Shades of color can be warm or cool. Using contrasting colors can bring life and excitement to your Web site, where varying shades of the same color can provide a different sense of depth. Contrasting colors can be used effectively to bring attention to important areas of your site. When one color dominates and the other is used sparingly as an accent, you can draw attention to certain elements of your site. Think about your history topic and the tone you want to provide. To choose your colors, you may want to draw from a particular color in an image you will feature prominently. There are times when you'll need a little variation, such as a little lighter or a tonal variation of a prominent color.

Footnotes can be viewed as pop-ups, either in the sidebar or in the middle of the page, or appearing when the mouse rolls over the number. See http://www.archiva.net/footnote/csspopup.htm for styling CSS tips.

Using different shades and tones of color can add a layer of texture and depth to your Web design. Tonal variations (play with opacity and fill layers to achieve this) may help in creating drop shadows or hover colors. You can add sepia tone to an image to make it look older, or you can add spot color to highlight certain things in an image or tie in your design theme. For help with blending colors to find different shades, see http://meyerweb.com/eric/ tools/color-blend/.

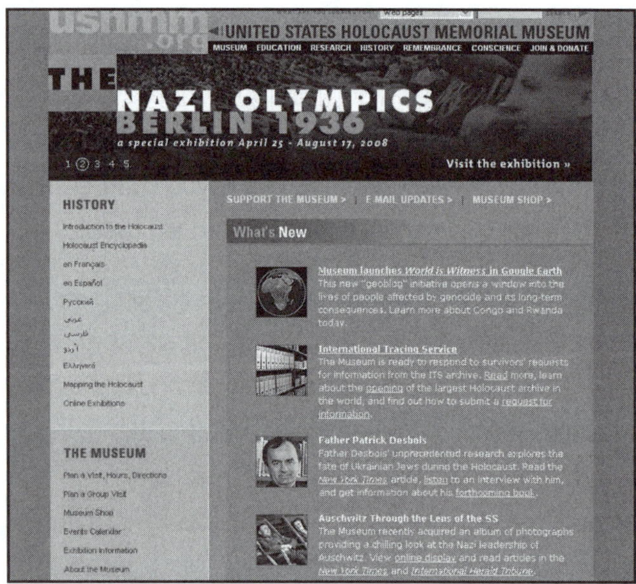

The United States Holocaust Memorial Museum uses blues, grays, and browns that are appropriate for its serious topic. http://www.ushmm.org/

Color also facilitates readability and draws attention to certain aspects of your site. You should use rich colors like red and yellow sparingly, and generally only for items you really wish to emphasize. Use different colors rather than different shapes to distinguish features on a page. Beware of the negative effects of certain highly contrasting colors placed next to each other (such as green and red), as well as the off-putting optical illusions created, for instance, by a series of parallel lines. If navigational elements have color at all, make sure their hues don't distract viewers from focusing on the main content of the page.

COLOR TIPS

- ***Use color to direct your focus.*** If you use a more neutral palette, with lighter shades of colors, your viewers will focus on your history rather than on your bright colors. Do not overuse color.
- ***Use color to organize.*** Use color to differentiate the layers or levels of your Web site. Be consistent and don't use too many different colors—rather, play with shades of the same colors.
- ***Use color to simplify.*** Too many words, images, and colors can create a lot of visual noise on your Web site. If your Web site is too busy, simplify your color palette.

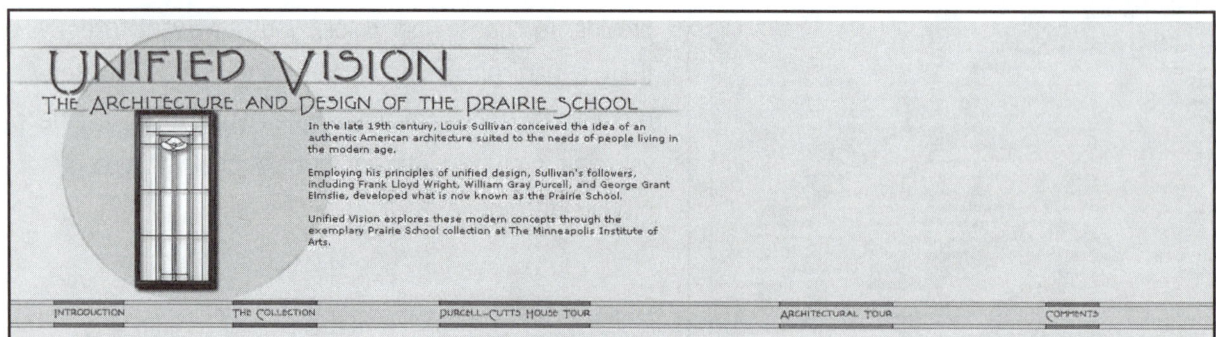

The Minneapolis Institute of Art's Unified Vision: The Architecture and Design of the Prairie School utilizes colors used by Frank Lloyd Wright in his design. The subtle nature shades hearken to Wright's nature motif, with good use of shades and variants. http://www.artsmia.org/unified-vision/purcell-cutts-house/

Multimedia Design

As you select images and documents to insert on your Web site, think about how you want to present them. Do you want to use a mash-up from another Web site to personalize a map or a time line for your site? Do you want to provide an image of a handwritten document or the typed transcript or both? A digital image of a document can showcase unique attributes, such as notes in the margin, personal handwriting, misspellings, and editing. They can also be harder to read, making it more challenging for the viewer to understand the source and your reason for including it.

One way to present multiple images is to use thumbnails that users can click into larger views. Placing a series of pertinent images in 75 × 75 pixel spaces allows you to maintain consistency and a clean presentation without compromising the individual power of the image. You feel as though you are in a museum gallery, and yet the Web experience allows you to have a more intimate experience with each image by clicking on it.

For both audio and video, you may want to add a time stamp to show how long a segment runs (remember to keep it to 45 seconds or less for each clip) and the total size of the multimedia file in megabytes, so visitors know what to expect before they click. Audio and video files should also tie into your overall design theme. Whatever special effects, images, maps, graphics, or audio and video files you decide to add to your Web site, remember to connect them to your thesis.

Ask yourself:

- How do these items help promote my topic?
- How will such effects persuade the user of my thesis?
- Do all my files and links work?

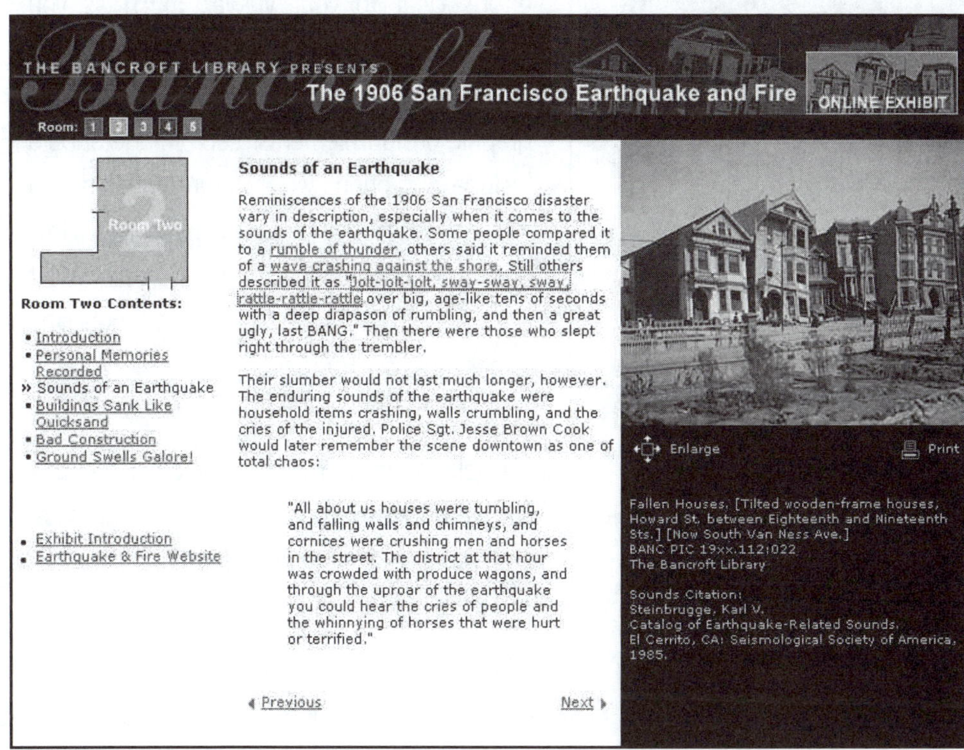

The Bancroft Library's Web site on the San Francisco earthquake of 1906 displays a photograph that can be enlarged with a citation. Viewers can link to audio files (thunder, waves, and other earthquake noises), as well as read sound analysis in the body text.
http://bancroft.berkeley.edu/collections/earthquakeandfire/exhibit/room02_item02.html

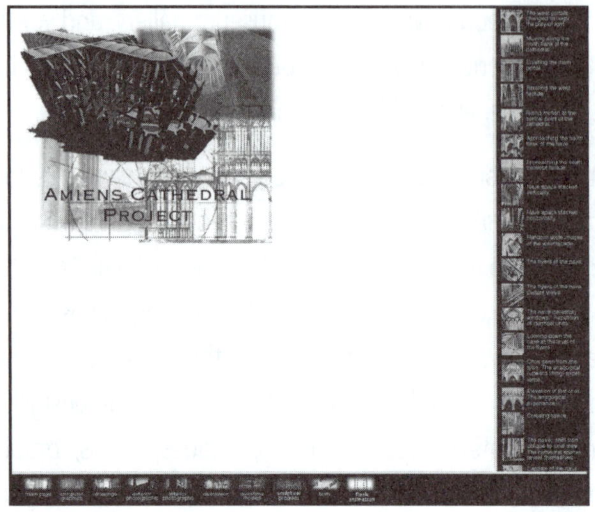

Columbia University's Media Center for Art History showcases images using thumbnails. The viewer can click for a larger view and explanation.http://www.learn.columbia.edu/Mcahweb/index-frame.html

Smith College's Vistas Gallery makes good use of thumbnails to detail valuable chronological information. http://www.smith.edu/vistas/vistas_web/gallery/gallery_main.htm

EDITING IMAGES

To get the perfect look for your Web site, you can use photo-editing software to manipulate your images. Make a copy of the original images on which to experiment. That way you can always go back to the original version should something get lost or altered beyond repair. You can crop, adjust brightness or contrast, and resize. Always keep in mind the theme of your site and your thesis, and think about how your images can reflect that. Remember that you cannot make an image bigger without losing sharpness and quality, but you can always make an image smaller. If you alter a historic image in any way and present it as documented evidence, whether by cropping, removing something, or enhancing the color, be sure to make your efforts clear to your viewer, much as you would add an ellipses (. . .) in altering quoted text, unless the picture is used as part of your graphic design elements. Each image should include a caption. Try to be interpretive and not just descriptive in your caption text. How does this image connect to your thesis? What does it tell the viewer specifically about the larger topic or argument?

FINAL WEB SITE CONSTRUCTION DETAILS

The NHD Web site http://www.nhd.org/ProjectCategories.htm has detailed information about Web site materials and construction as well as helpful tips on Web site design.

When all of the pieces—text, images and multimedia (if any), and navigation—come together in a well laid-out and structured history Web site, the results can be both visually appealing and informative. Make sure the design between your home page and internal pages is consistent; use the same colors, fonts, and design tactics. Check all links.

For the most current National History Day instructions on submission rules, you should refer to the Web site at http://www.nhd.org/Website.htm.

As you work, be sure to save your Web site often. You may want to back up your work for safe keeping.

SOLID DESIGN TIPS

Keep it simple. Don't waste too much time on bells and whistles. Tell your story and tell it straight.

Borrow ideas from other Web sites. Find design elements that work and imitate them on your Web site. It's kind of like doing historical research: find what the experts have done and do it, too. Just remember to give credit where credit is due.

Make sure every element of your design points back to your thesis, topic, and/or time period. There should be a conscious reason for every choice you make about color, typeface, or graphics.

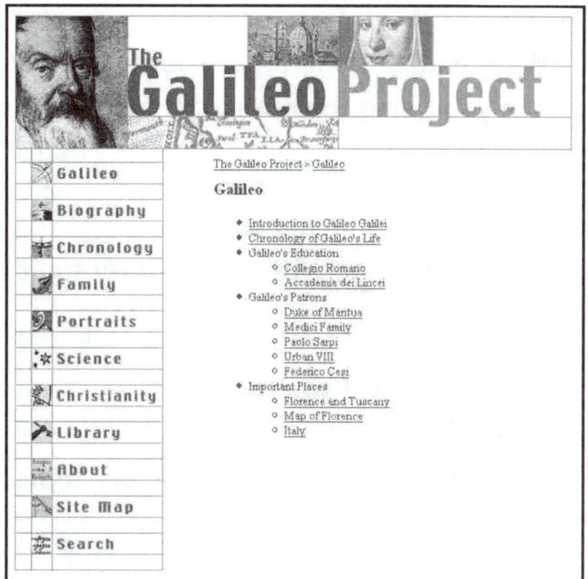

The Galileo Project at Rice University draws from its theme in every aspect of the site's design: navigation, color, and layout. http://galileo.rice.edu/galileo.html

VISIT HISTORY WEB SITES

One way to start thinking about your Web site is to visit history Web sites and look at how professionals design them. This will give you ideas for displaying your research findings and let you see how Web site developers present findings.

Here are a few questions that will help you think about what makes a successful Web site.

- Does the title catch your attention and summarize the subject of the Web site?
- Are the documents, photos, or objects displayed clearly related to the Web site's topic? Or is it hard to see how the various materials relate to each other and to the topic of the Web site?
- Who is the intended audience for the Web site? Is it primarily for children? For students? For people who enjoy the subject as a hobby (like stamp collectors or antique automobile lovers)? For professional historians? For the general public? How can you tell?
- How did the Web designer use color and design on the Web site? Do the colors and design make you want to explore the Web site further? Do they seem appropriate or connected to the theme? Do they overwhelm the content of the Web site?
- Does the entire Web site work as a whole, or does it seem disorganized and unclear? Are the subsections linked to the main home page? Do all the links work? Is the content stable—does the appearance change if the page is refreshed in the browser?

- What is the template for your Web site?
  Are you going to create one or use a template from a prebuilt program?

- What colors will you use?
  How do they go with your history topic?

- What fonts will you use?
  What size?
  How do they go with your history topic?

  - Main title:
  - Header:
  - Text:
  - Quotations:
  - Captions:
  - Footnotes:

- How will the design on your pages be consistent across all the pages?

QUALITIES OF A GOOD NHD WEB SITE

Here are the qualities a judge will use to evaluate your NHD Web site. After you create your Web site, go through this list and ask yourself if you've met the criteria or incorporated the information into your project.

Historical Quality: 60%

The historical quality of your Web site is by far the most important criteria.

- ☐ **My Web site is historically accurate:** All the information in my Web site is true to the best of my knowledge.
- ☐ **I show analysis and interpretation:** My Web site doesn't just recount facts or tell a story. I interpret and analyze my topic. My Web site has a strong central thesis or argument that I prove. I can point to where I state my thesis in my Web site.
- ☐ **I place my topic in its historical context:** My topic didn't take place in isolation. I make sure to place my topic into historical context—the intellectual, physical, social, and cultural setting for my topic.
- ☐ **My project shows wide, balanced research and I use available primary sources:** These ideas all relate to the research behind your NHD Web site. Judges will look carefully at your bibliography to learn more about your research process. They want to see that you investigated multiple perspectives about your topic and that you looked at all sides of an issue. They are looking for research using both primary and secondary sources and want to see that you used a variety of source types.

Relation to Theme: 20%

- ☐ **I clearly relate my topic to the theme:** My theme connection is clear in my Web site itself.
- ☐ **I demonstrate the significance of my topic in history and draw conclusions:** My Web site does more than just describe my topic. I explain why my topic is important in history or demonstrate its significance.

Clarity of Presentation: 20%

- ☐ **My Web site and written materials are original, clear, appropriate, and organized:** I have an organized and well-written project. I was careful to avoid plagiarism and I have double-checked spelling and grammar in my Web site, process paper, and bibliography.
- ☐ **My Web site has visual impact, uses multimedia effectively, and actively involves the viewer:** I thought about the overall design and organization of my Web site. I chose multimedia and interactive elements to help viewers understand my topic and prove my argument.

Before turning in your Web site for judging, triple-check your site to make sure it works. Go through the pages on several different browsers and computers. Make sure that all your links work and that your images show up. Have your friends and teachers also check your links and multimedia files from their computers. Give yourself plenty of time to test the site so you can correct any problems you may find.

As a Web designer, the burden is yours to make sure your Web site is in working order. Neither the judge nor the contest coordinator will fix broken page links, images, and so on. If elements of your site are not working, that doesn't mean your entry will be disqualified. The judges will use the paper version of your site to try to understand your Web site. The judges will, however, take nonworking elements of your site into consideration as they evaluate the clarity of presentation of your project.

When evaluating NHD Web sites, judges should be able to find all the information about your topic within your Web site. The Web site has to stand on its own. Have someone who has never seen your Web site look at it (e.g., a friend, teacher, neighbor). Without saying anything, let them read through the entire Web site. Then, ask them a few questions to see if you communicated your argument clearly: What am I trying to prove in my Web site? What evidence have I shown to support that argument? What do you like about my Web site? What is confusing to you?

WRITING YOUR PROCESS PAPER AND ANNOTATED BIBLIOGRAPHY

In addition to creating your Web site, NHD requires you to turn in a process paper of no more than 500 words and an annotated bibliography. Your process paper needs to explain how and why you chose your topic, how you conducted your research, why you selected the Web site category, and how your Web site relates to the NHD theme. This does not count toward your 1,200-word limit.

Although the process paper for your Web site will be similar to process papers in the other categories, writing about your Web site gives you another opportunity to note why you found a document or image especially important to display. You might also want to state how you used different design elements to present a certain argument or highlight a primary source.

Annotated bibliographies demonstrate the breadth and depth of your research to the judges. You need to cite each source that was useful to you, whether or not it was displayed on your Web site. For example, a journal article may have raised an important question, or a history professor may have suggested a manuscript collection for you to investigate. Your annotated bibliography needs to include these sources and show why they were helpful to you. The annotated bibliography must be included as an integral part of the Web site with a link from the home page. It does not count toward your 1,200-word limit.

Web sites often use a broader variety of sources than the more traditional paper. Be sure to cite these nontraditional sources as well as the books, articles, newspapers, and archives you use. If you use photographs on your Web site, cite them in your bibliography. If recorded music gives your Web site a sense of time and place, the recording and the artist must be cited.

Specific rules and an example of an entry for an annotated bibliography can be found on the NHD Web site http://www.nhd.org/EssentialInfo.htm.

SUBMISSION

For up-to-date submission procedures, please visit http://www.nhd.org.

GLOSSARY

absolute link
Defines the specific location of the file including the full address, the protocol to use to get the document, the server to get it from, the directory it is located in, and the name of the document itself. A relative link, in contrast, includes a shortened directory.

<ahref="http://www.domain.com/pagename.html"></a>

archive
A repository for historical documents, artifacts, or images. Some archives digitize their collections and make them available online. Some archives make finding aids outlining their collections available online. Some archives make their catalogs available online. Others have limited resources and do not have much of an online presence, so you will have to visit their facilities in person.

artifact
A historical object. Often these objects are found in museums or archives, but they can also be owned by private individuals or families. For example, your family may have your great-grandfather's World War II army uniform, or a neighbor may have the passport from when her mother came to the United States from Italy. Photographs of artifacts are often displayed as part of history Web sites.

browser See Web browser

context
The background, time, or environment that shapes a historical event or the life of an individual.

CSS (cascading style sheet)
A standard for specifying the appearance of text and other elements. CSS is typically used to provide a single "library" of styles that are used over and over throughout a large number of related documents, as in a Web site. A CSS file might specify that all numbered lists are to appear in italics. By changing that single specification the look of a large number of documents can be easily changed.

database
An electronic collection of historical sources, images, sounds, records, bibliographies, or other historical data.

dead or broken link
A URL or Web address to a Web site that no longer exists or cannot be accessed.

digital image (e.g.,jpeg, tiff, gif, png)
A digital image is a representation of a two-dimensional image as a finite set of digital values, called pixels (short for "picture elements"). Typically, the pixels are stored in computer memory as a raster image or raster map, a two-dimensional array of small integers. These values are often transmitted or stored in a compressed form (e.g., images with a document type of .jpeg, .png, or .gif)

domain name system (DNS)
This is a system that stores information about host names and domain names on networks, such as the Internet. Most importantly, it provides an IP (Internet protocol) address for each host name and lists the mail exchange servers accepting email for each domain. The DNS forms a vital part of the Internet, because hardware requires IP addresses to perform routing, but humans use host names and domain names, for example in URLs and e-mail addresses.

domain name
The unique name that identifies an Internet site. Domain names always have two or more parts, separated by dots. The part on the left is the most specific, and the part on the right is the most general. For example, the domain name of the Web site located at http://www.loc.gov/exhibits/gadd/4403.html is "loc.gov."

fair use
The fair-use doctrine is a body of law and court decisions that provides for limitations and exceptions to copyright protection in the United States. Fair use attempts to balance the interests of copyright holders with the public interest in the wider distribution and use of creative works by allowing certain limited uses that would otherwise be considered infringement of copyright.

GIF (graphic interchange format)
This is a file format on the Internet that allows browsers to display graphics. The .gif format is more appropriate for line drawings or maps because it provides more precise image definition. The .jpg or .jpeg format is preferred to the .gif format for color photographs because the .gif format allows only 256 colors.

historical perspective
An individual's point of view on a historic event, movement, or person; the "place" from which an individual views that event or person. This includes not only geographic location (e.g., looking at a battle from a hill above the fight or on the battlefield) or individual outlook (e.g., a father may have a different perspective than his daughter about her date) but also intellectual, political, economic, social, religious, or other perspective (e.g., the different perspectives of workers and a manager on a strike, or of a liberal Democrat from a conservative Republican on a bill in Congress).

home page
The Web page that serves as a starting point or table of contents for a Web site. It can also mean a personal Web site in its entirety.

host
Also called a "server," it is a computer that holds the Web page and is connected to the Internet so other users (called "clients") can access it. NHD will host your Web site.

HTML (hypertext markup language)
The basic code in which most Web pages are written.

HTTP (hypertext transport protocol or hypertext transfer protocol)
The method in which Web pages are sent from the host to the user's browser.

hyperlink or hypertext
Provides the ability to link or move in a nonlinear way from one place to another. System for transferring viewers from one Web page or location to another. A hyperlink can be image or text, whereas hypertext refers to text that are hyperlinks.

icon
A graphic symbol on which the user can click to go to another document or part of the Web site.

interactive
A device in a Web site that allows the visitor to participate. These include but are not limited to hyperlinks, pop-ups, and audio selections.

IP address
An Internet protocol or IP address is a unique number computers use to refer to each other when sending information through the Internet. This allows machines passing on the information on behalf of the sender to know where to send it next. Converting to these numbers from the more human-readable form of domain addresses, such as www.example.com, is done via the domain name system. The process of conversion is known as resolution of domain names.

ISP (Internet service provider)
An institution that provides access to the Internet in some form.

JPEG (joint photographic experts group)
A file format that allows browsers to display graphics. The .jpg or .jpeg format is preferred to the .gif format for color photographs because the .gif format allows only 256 colors. The .gif format is more appropriate for line drawings or maps because it provides more precise image definition.

kerning
Space between letters. Kerning that is too tight or too loose can be problematic. Make sure your text can breath, but don't adjust your kerning to make it difficult to read.

leading
Line spacing in text, that is, the amount of space between lines. In the days of mechanical typesetting, leading referred to the strips of lead used to create space between the lines of text. Long lines of text may require extra leading. Bold face or sans serif fonts require more leading. Leading affects the density of your page. If your page seems dark, try adding more leading to lighten the visual effect and readability.

mash-up
A Web page or site made by automatically combining content from other sources, usually by using material available via RSS feeds and/or REST interfaces.

MPEG (motion picture experts group)
This is a standard format for audio and video files frequently found on the Internet.

MP3
Based on MPEG technology, this is a file format for high-quality audio.

narrative
An account of a historical event or the biography of an individual structured in such a way that it tells a story. A narrative can be presented in chronological order or by thematic organization, but it usually has a strong sense of sequential order.

OCR (optical character recognition)
The mechanical or electronic translation of images of handwritten or printed text (usually captured by a scanner) into machine-editable text.

oral history
History based on oral interviews of surviving witnesses or participants.

padding
The distance between the border of an HTML element and the content within it.

PDF (portable document format)
A common format for sharing formatted documents over the Internet. Users need the free Adobe Acrobat software in order to view the document.

podcast
An audio or video recording that is converted into an .mp3 file so that it can be downloaded and played on portable audio or video devices such as Apple's popular iPod.

primary source
Historical materials directly related to a topic by time or participation. These may take the form of an original diary entry, a historical photograph, a map, a newspaper, or a petition.

pull quote
A small selection of text "pulled out and quoted" in a larger typeface. It stands out from the accompanying text. The pull quote my be framed by

lines or blank space, placed within the body text, or placed in an empty column. Also known as a lift-out quote or a call out.

public domain
Accessible to all, not protected by copyright. Internationally, the public domain is the body of creative works and other knowledge—writing, artwork, music, science, inventions, and other—in which no person or organization has any proprietary interest. Such works and inventions are considered part of the public's cultural heritage, and anyone can use and build on them without restriction.

QTVR (QuickTime virtual reality)
A format for viewing a three-dimensional or panoramic view.

relative link
Does not include the full file address—http:// and domain name—as for an absolute link. The server knows where the current document is and will assume the link is connected to the current folder.

<a href="pagename.html"></a>

A backslash at the beginning of the address will direct the server to return to the root directory.

<a href="/Chapter2/Part1/page23.html">here</a>

secondary source
Historical materials on a topic that are not related by time or participation. For example, books and article by historians or interviews with professors are usually secondary sources.

server
In computing, a server is a computer software application that carries out some task on behalf of users. This is usually divided into file serving, allowing users to store and access files on a common computer, and application serving, where the software runs a computer program to carry out some task for the users. The term is now also used to mean the physical computer on which the software runs.

storyboard
A visual outline or sketch of your Web site. A simple storyboard may be a flowchart, a table, or an outline, whereas a more complex storyboard allows you to draw out details of each element as well. A storyboard helps you visualize details and how pages link.

streaming media
Audio or video that "streams" continuously through a player such as Real Audio or Windows Media Player instead of first requiring a download.

upload
To send a file from one, usually smaller, computer to a server or host.

URL (uniform resource locator)
The "address" or "location" of a Web site. URLs are in the form hostname.domain, for example, bedfordstmartins.com, and are usually preceded by http://.

Web browser or browser
A web browser is a software package that enables a user to display and interact with HTML documents hosted by Web servers. The largest networked collection of hypertext documents is known as the World Wide Web. Common Web browsers include Internet Explorer, Netscape Navigator, Safari, and Firefox. For purposes of the NHD competition, your Web site should be created for use with Microsoft Internet Explorer.

A more extensive glossary may be found at http://www.matisse.net/files/glossary.html.

ABOUT THE AUTHOR

Jennifer Reeder is a doctoral student in American history at George Mason University in Fairfax, Virginia. She works at the Center for History and New Media where she is involved with several history Web sites, including the National History Education Clearinghouse, History Matters, World History Matters, Object of History, and several Teaching American History grants. She is the editorial director for Clio Visualizing History, an educational history Web site. She received an MA in history and archival management from New York University and has worked at the Brooklyn Museum archives, the Gilder Lehrman Collection at the New York Historical Society, the American Jewish Historical Society, and the Joseph Fielding Smith Institute for LDS History at Brigham Young University.

ACKNOWLEDGMENTS

Thanks go to the Center for History and New Media, with special assistance from Kelly Schrum, Lee Ann Ghajar, Sheila Brennan, Jeremy Boggs, Jon Lester, and Ken Albers.

Additional thanks go to Steve Cure, Eleanor Greene, Mills Kelly, Pat Melville, Thomas Thurston, and of course, Cathy Gorn and Katrina Dodro, who make it all happen.

ADDITIONAL RESOURCES

BOOKS

Cohen, Daniel J. and Roy Rosenzweig. *Digital History: A Guide to Gathering, Preserving, and Presenting the Past on the Web.* University of Pennsylvania Press, 2005. Available online at http://chnm.gmu.edu/digitalhistory/index.php

Williams, Robin and John Tollett. *The Non-Designer's Web Book: An Easy Guide to Creating, Designing, and Posting Your Own Web Site.* Peachpit Press, 1997.

WEBSITES

Typography:

Typography Matters: http://www.alistapart.com/stories/typography/

Scholarship on the Web: Managing and Presenting Footnotes and Endnotes: http://www.archiva.net/footnote/

Color:

Color Strategy: http://www.ideabook.com/tutorials/web_design/color_strategy.html#more

Natural Selections: Colors Found in Nature and Interface Design: http://www.boxesandarrows.com/view/natural_selections_colors_found_in_nature_and_interface_design

Colour Tools: http://www.clagnut.com/blog/260/

Photographic Palettes: http://24ways.org/2006/photographic-palettes

CSS:

Floatutorial: Simple Tutorials on CSS Floats: http://css.maxdesign.com.au/floatutorial/index.htm

Listutorial: Simple Tutorials on CSS Based Lists http://css.maxdesign.com.au/listutorial/index.htm

Design:

Guidelines for Visualizing Links: http://www.useit.com/alertbox/20040510.html

Scholarship on the Web: Matting, Engravings, and Line Art: http://www.archiva.net/engravings/index.htm

Super-Easy Blendy Backgrounds: http://www.alistapart.com/articles/supereasyblendys

That Wicked Worn Look: http://www.cameronmoll.com/archives/000024.html

Webmonkey: The Web Developer's Resource: http://www.webmonkey.com/

ONLINE HISTORY RESEARCH

Gilder Lehrman Institute of American History: http://gilderlehrman.org/

History Matters: http://historymatters.gmu.edu/

Library of Congress: http://www.loc.gov/index.html

National Archives and Records Administration: http://www.archives.gov/index.html

Women in World History: http://chnm.gmu.edu/wwh/index.html

World History Sources: http://chnm.gmu.edu/worldhistorysources/index.html

NHD wishes to thank the sponsors of How to Create a Historical Web Site:

ABC-CLIO Schools

CENTER for HISTORY and NEW MEDIA

NOTES

NOTES

NOTES

NOTES